SHAKING THE OLD OAK TREE

One man's marketing journey as an agent
of change in the world of finance

BRUCE SOUTHERDEN

Copyright © Bruce Southerden 2022

All rights reserved. No part of this publication may be reproduced, distributed or transmitted in any form or by any means including photocopying, recording, or other electronic or mechanical methods without the prior written permission of the publisher except in the case of brief quotations embodied in critical reviews and certain other non-commercial uses permitted by copyright law. The author and publisher do not assume and hereby disclaim any liability to any party for any loss, damage, or disruption caused by misinformation, errors or omissions whether such errors or omissions result from negligence, accident, or any other cause. Adherence to all applicable laws and regulations, including international, federal, state, and local regulations governing professional licensing, business practices, advertising, and all other aspects of doing business in the US, Australia or any other jurisdiction is the sole responsibility of the reader and consumer. Neither the author nor the publisher assumes any responsibility or liability whatsoever on behalf of the consumer or reader of this material.

ISBN: 978-0-6454203-1-9

To my very best friends Charlie and Rasa

And to so many of my loyal colleagues over the years who always did their best to help make a difference

Contents

Foreword	5
Author's note	7
Start here	8
Out of the blocks	13
A beginning	18
The country life	20
Big change	28
The advertising agency	33
A brave new world	36
Next hill	41
Back home	49
Stepping into marketing	52
Exploring	69
Next match	74
Lion eats zebra	83
Getting the board on board	87
The open road	90
Out of the frying pan	92
At the casino with your money	98
Freedom	102
The directors' chapter	104
Match point	107
Postscript	109

Foreword

This is a book of stories. About how a simple life grew into a serious marketing career in a strange world where marketing was not seen to be needed. I was an agent of change in an industry that didn't want to change.

My intention is to present a snapshot of what life was like before everything took off post-war with some tales you might enjoy and some ideas for those who strive to do more, those of you keen to meet challenges armed with a better knowledge of battle lines and more confidence in trying to make things happen. I also want to help those just setting out on their own marketing roads, which will all have potholes, twists and turns.

But wherever you work and whatever your job description is, my hope is that this book will give you an insight into how the simple concept of marketing works, and how it is very often taken for granted that anything can be done or created, and promotion will fix any problems that come up between seller and buyer. It won't.

Let's simplify things even further for a moment. Every other animal on our planet survives by eating other species. We also happen to be animals that make things – whilst also eating other species.

Our very existence as humans depends on the process of bartering with others in exchange for things valuable to us. Lots of wonderful stuff. Heaps more of rubbish for temporary enjoyment or to help destroy our world, carelessly or intentionally. An unstoppable train accelerating to a not-so-far-away destination yet unclear.

It's not for me to question all this. I'd still rather be me than a lizard under the sharp eye of a crow. Or an ant on a footpath.

So, let's agree being human is good. But what I want to invite you to reflect on is that the business of making and bartering, the constant backwards and forwards of goods and services, has one element sometimes overlooked or missing in action: marketing. Not the idea of marketing many of us have grown up with, but the essence of creating and doing for the simple purpose of getting another party to join us in the barter. How that other party can be convinced, cajoled or tricked into taking part is a whole other subject for another book.

My focus here is to shed light on that basic other side of the equation of creating anything to barter: *necessary acceptance by someone else*. Whatever you're offering must satisfy their wants or needs.

Over the course of my long career in marketing I have often said that marketing really boils down to two simple words: common sense. This might seem trite, but take a moment to look around and you'll see examples everywhere of the failure of common sense in what people try to sell to others and the way they try to do that. Products and packaging that appear to have design flaws, at times confirmed when new, improved versions follow later. Promotions that miss the mark, aiming to be different or attract attention using devices that overshadow the products themselves and the reasons to buy them. Opportunities to make changes that can have positive market effects that aren't taken advantage of. I'll give you some examples in this book. Relatively small things like differences in how companies deal with customer calls – one enables call-backs to save waiting, an obvious benefit, yet you wonder why their competitors have not introduced such an improvement or recognised that their customers also endure long waiting periods.

Finally, a word for you if you are in the so-called new generation. I realise that the old times can be of little interest to some, whilst others do feel a need to know what things used to be like. Hopefully, my efforts to paint a little of the picture of what it was like before you joined us will be of some help.

Author's note

The names of a few of the people in this book have been changed to protect their privacy. I have also taken the liberty of adding a bit of colour to a few of the stories to help with their telling.

My hope is that you will enjoy this book and take from it what you wish. Life is the biggest gift to every soul on our planet. The packaging might be different for each one of us. Sometimes glossy, less so for most of us. Some people are destined to live on the edge with little choice but to accept the hand they were dealt. Others seem to arrive with a free pass.

Every one of us has a story worth telling. And whatever road we're travelling on it's not where you start that matters most. It's how you leave when the bell rings and, along the way, how you have adopted and held to values that count – using your gift well in the community we all share. I hope these stories from my journey help to guide you on yours.

Start here

Please don't think this is an autobiography. There won't be stories about my 38-second dip in icy waters off Antarctica. Or the time I noticed, on a walking safari in Kenya, that my Maasai guide was wearing Billabong boardshorts under his warrior robes when he reached for the mobile phone in his pocket to take a call from his village. Or getting a fright when I woke up a bull shark in the sand twenty feet below me while I was scuba diving off Smoky Cape on the NSW north coast. Or hearing dingo pups howling five miles away in the silence of midnight in the desert. Or tucking in to a breakfast of bacon and eggs in the Metropole in Moscow in the 1970s – served in a bowl with a soup spoon.

No. I'm not Andre Agassi and unlike him I've done nothing in my life to make anyone sit up and take notice. Everyone has their own lives and I've got mine. People need to know about the lives of stars. Not us. I'm not even as nice as Andre. Far from it.

So if it's not an autobiography, where does it go in the bookstore or the library? What kind of book is this? Answer: it's your Racing Guide, if you're in the Marketing Race, filled with things you need to know, things that aren't in the usual handbooks. For others I hope you'll find it interesting how marketing works, or doesn't.

I've said to many marketing students over the years: pick up your degree, but always remember there's no end to marketing in any place you'll ever work. It's the lifeblood of all business, everywhere. Marketing is also a curious thing.

To use just one example, it costs the airlines pretty much the same per second or minute to fly you from, say, Sydney to Melbourne, whether you go with Virgin or Jetstar. Lease costs, fuel, landing and parking, staff, cleaning, everything. Yet your flight might cost twice as much on Monday morning as it does on Sunday afternoon. Why? The usual answer is market demand. The more people who want to fly on one day, the cheaper the flights will be on that day.

So, let's see if different pricing works when buying a car, with most car purchases made on Saturdays. Should post offices start charging less early in the week before people panic over getting their parcels away? Is there a day of the week when vacuum cleaners should be half price?

Then again there are other things consumers just go along with. Take the Jetstar attendant with the luggage scales as you first walk into the airport terminal. If your carry-on bag is half a kilo over the limit she'll hit you for the price of the suitcase. You don't go near her and take it with you. Then wait for the flight call and walk through anyway. No surcharge at the gate because it's a late call and they wave you through.

An imperfect marketing world all over and as I'll show you in this book marketing is sometimes absent altogether in the world of finance.

Let's take airline pricing a bit further.

The Australian Competition and Consumer Commission (ACCC) and Fair Trading bodies in each state may have looked over the scene with both Jetstar and Virgin and perceived that some flights were loss-makers but still had to operate with schedules and the need to get aircraft to other airports for following flights. So airlines needed to make that up somewhere. No way to adjust prices because other flights had to be priced to compensate. Not that fair on customers, but it should be up to the players to compete and when that happens customers should win.

Imagine Flight Centre boss Graham Turner taking up as head of marketing at Virgin. First thing he'd be looking to ditch the Virgin name and save a quarter billion or so in royalties paid to Sir Richard Branson over the next two decades in return for value he provides, if any, in terms of helping to run a profitable airline in Australia. Then he could rebrand the outfit as Flight Centre Air. Next with a look at the competitive picture he might decide to end the taint of collusion with the other crowd starting next month and go hard. Fix a set price for all flights any hour any day Sydney to Melbourne, Brisbane to Adelaide or wherever. It's not a new concept: I still remember when flights in the US cost a hundred dollars standard, whichever city you flew to or from and whatever day or time of day you travelled.

Sure, prices for flights at the cheaper times would go up, but the scavenging at the other end would cease and, take a wild guess, people would not only know where they stood but there would be a real point of difference between the airlines. The masses would be greatly impressed. Loyalty would follow.

Systems would be easier and customers wouldn't need three hours to work out the cheapest flights when they book online. People wouldn't see flight prices changing on-screen before their eyes while making their bookings. The benefits would flow on to travel agents, ticketing, everywhere.

You could also structure the pricing model with scope for promotional discounting, say $50 off for every second booking for Valentine's Day. Or Thursday specials to drive more traffic into that day of the week so you have more capacity for the Friday afternoon weekenders. Simple deals that would be easy for the market to understand and believe rather than the mess we have now. Also, any upward adjustment against rising fuel costs, for example, could be presented to the public as reasonable instead of secret surprises hidden in unfathomable pricing detail.

The simple savings in not needing two hundred staff to work on different prices for all the flights and keep changing them every ten minutes, every day, on some set of traffic algorithms, would be enough to offset a sizeable increase in promotion to support the new structure.

Let Jetstar live with its self-made problems. No more terminal gouging with extra cost for that half kilogram over the weight limit of your checked-in luggage (even though one passenger weighs 65kg and the next one 105kg) or the 22 per cent surcharge to change seats – or double that to change flights because you got stuck in traffic getting to the airport or just changed your mind about flying that day.

The first point I'm trying to make here before we go further is that all of this is marketing. It's exciting and creates results wherever you happen to be. Airlines or places where a fancy bottle of perfume costs more than the perfume inside it and you're struggling at the upper end of the market. Or a new way into the real estate market or selling fridges on a 6-year replacement basis to lock customers into your brand. The company wins when marketing is there to battle things out with production, distribution, finance, human resources and all the other team members. But not so much when it's just advertising, PR and promotion.

No company is going to get that input, new ideas or creativity in this sense from the people with double degrees in accounting, chemical engineering, human resource management, IT or even business. It comes from having constant marketing focus.

My second point is about marketing in finance, the theme of this book. To me that's even more exciting because of its scope. Businesses in the whole finance sector have improved, but their learning period has been shorter so there's a way to go yet. Also, they have a huge advantage – they don't have to play with tangibles like hotel chains, cars or boats, household cleaners or drinks, all of which make things more complex.

Marketing in finance is like a huge net you can use to go fishing every day – and you can change your net tomorrow if you want. Whereas you can't with stuff on the shelves or in the showroom. And you're not confined to one sector of the global market, like only those using cosmetics or those needing crop fertiliser. Finance is the global everywhere market, allowing for differences in richer and poorer regions of course.

Lastly, be patient with these first pages until the shoots pop up above the soil. I've included this chapter just to show how beginnings begin, not necessarily with a plan for the rest of your life carved in stone.

If I'd said I grew up, went to school, learned not a lot and then mainly by rote, got a job in advertising as mail boy and became a marketing guru, how do you think that would have gone down? Not well, I suspect, unless I was setting out to write a same-old marketing manual.

Of course I have included some of my life story. For two reasons: for you to enjoy and to twist a few marketing angles into the book in a more interesting way than the usual "go here, now there" instructions, presented in the right order. That's not for me. I couldn't write like that and you wouldn't want to read it. This way I hope you will.

∼

Before we get started, I should explain why I present finance as a world so resistant to change, at least in terms of marketing, one that I unwittingly entered as an agent of change. In the following pages I write about the difference between finance and other industries where, as I mentioned above, tangible products impose multiple constraints on a marketing culture. You could call it simply evolution since Henry Ford, which is certainly true, but there is one clear factor beyond that. It is the difference between two *types* of product: one requiring constant nurturing of the consumer, the other (finance) not so much, although that's now changing.

With virtually any tangible product, customers pay and their money goes into that year's turnover figure. All done except for some who continue to pay on a maintenance contract or subscription or some other arrangement. Transaction completed. Even leasing and other payment schemes are completed transactions with financing being just part of the sale. You keep needing customers for next year's turnover, repeat or brand new. Ongoing marketing isn't optional but necessary, otherwise you fall behind in the marketplace, retailers refuse to put your goods on the eye-level shelves, your brand becomes overshadowed, competitors see weakness. Everything.

Now let's look at banks. Their customers aren't one-off buyers of products. Income from them translates into turnover figures year after year. As long as they remain or are replaced by others. Of course, in its broadest sense marketing plays its part in terms of location of branches, ability of staff and quality of service, but you could say that generally if a bank or other financial organisation keeps in line with its competitors and market expectations and has a good customer base, it has few worries. It can hold its own with close connections in the marketplace. Competition is possible by simply adjusting interest rates or lending policies. Advertising beyond support for a new branch opening and such needs is more or less optional. You could run a media campaign for a while to feel good and expect to be in a comfortable slot in any brand recall study, which may or may not cause your customers to stay or leave you. Keeping up with the competition.

It's no wonder, then, that in all my years of marketing I regularly witnessed management and boards of financial institutions failing to see the need to change tack or consider any more substantial investment to attack the market and grow their market share significantly. They had their customers and they knew how to keep them. Old oak trees all. But they were on the brink of change. They just didn't know it yet.

Out of the blocks

I don't remember when I was born. In Toowoomba, west of Brisbane. In the late thirties, someone told me. Maybe I said at that moment, "Strap yourself in" – or I should have, now I come to think of it.

Growing up – even though growing up really never stops – my life was as ordinary as all the lives of all the other ordinary kids in ordinary families. Next door. Next street. Next suburb. Everywhere. We just thought we were normal.

Social life, for our family, I recall in two parts. Friends and relatives coming to our place, with days to prepare for the special occasion. Food in the ice chest under the house until we got the Kelvinator – watching the iceman when he comes with his horse and cart to make sure he brings two blocks down the side this week. Put the hessian around them in the top to last longer. Help with the shopping and don't get the beans if they're more than one and six pence.

The same going over to other houses. Friends or the home of my father's brother Les, who would entertain everyone with Ogden Nash recitals.

The first job I ever had was thanks to Les. He started his business with two others, making and selling backpacks for spraying, and I gave the floors and desks a wipe for a few hours on Saturday mornings in his office in Brisbane.

Sadly, his journey ended with him depending on care in a home and he couldn't even recognise any of us. A reminder for all of us choosing to think about things how precious the gift of life really is. Respect what you have because someone can take it away at any moment.

My two first heroes, my father and my Uncle Les. Both born before cars were invented. Before 1900. In their twenties when war broke out, single and earning a living somewhere – I know too little of that, and would have learned more by asking, if I'd had more of the wisdom that comes with age.

They took up an ex-soldiers' grant of bush acres near Stanthorpe in southern Queensland after the war and with just a horse, a cart and a few hand tools they cleared part of it. Then used the felled saplings to make a slab hut to sleep in and a yard for the horse. In winter the morning basin wash had to wait until near noon for ice to turn back to water. I imagine their days began with feeding the horse and a simple breakfast then to clearing, making the fire heap, picking stones and larger rocks from the Granite Belt earth and putting hoes in to break the soil for planting. Apple trees, or the hope of apples later. Seed planting the only way, no nurseries back then, but as soon as shoots sprang up the rabbits would get there first. Plant again. Feed the rabbits. Plant again. Feed the rabbits.

Tough years. Almost nothing to show for it. Eventually Les left to marry Doris in Brisbane and they walked off the plot with little to their names. My father went on the road as a travelling clothes fitter for Rothwells touring western Queensland towns I came to know later, like Blackall, Longreach and Isisford. If only I could have shared stories with him. At Tambo, another town, my father began his romance with Sister Emma Buetel, a nurse at the local hospital. Our family followed later.

As my own life unfolded I had no idea where it would lead. Our first car the Chev tourer needing a crank start at times. A long day's driving on holidays to an old cottage in Caloundra, on the coast. Or anywhere with good fishing. Boxes tied on the running boards and spare water to top up the radiator on the way. Upgrading to the grey Vauxhall with wind-up windows and pop-out "trafficators". More memories and things forgotten as I grew taller.

Snapshots from that time. The years of gathering around the big radio, and be quiet you kids, for news of how the war was going. The day Darwin was bombed. Cutting brown paper to put over the windows so we could switch on the lights during blackouts. Hearing warplane engines down at Eagle Farm every night. Probably doing practice runs at Brisbane's Story Bridge which wasn't lit up in those years for some reason. The walk down to Sandgate Road to watch the endless convoy of tanks and artillery on low loaders and other trucks with gear and waving soldiers of all the lower ranks heading north – two days and two nights it lasted. You'll understand that was not conducive to thinking where your life might take you or how to start your career. More conducive to optimism than forward planning. Let's get out of this hole first. Then we'll look around and see which way to run.

War over. We won. New life! Starting slowly, watching the price of the beans. Relatives or friends over occasionally or going there. No restaurants except in the city and "the Valley" and they were only for the rich and the big spenders. No chance of buying just a coffee even if there was somewhere to get it. Just the odd cafes with milkshakes, toast and cheese on a plate or something else fairly plain, like corned beef or fish and chips. OK for somewhere to hang but hardly something to look forward to. Is my life starting yet? No. Wait. We can't afford it yet.

No complaints. Not much neighbourhood gossip. Or arguing over the fence. People were mates with some and not as close to others and as things go, we were ordinary. The big guy with the greasy leather on his shoulder who came down the side of our house to change the toilet bins each week did the same for everyone in the street. Same with the man bringing our two bottles of milk. And the man with the baker's van behind his horse. And the iceman. All simple because no cars parked in the street, only visitors, so you'd always know who was coming to someone else's house across the road on a Sunday afternoon.

Noise and chaos were distant, beyond our suburban gaze. Generally confined to the pub down the road next to the cinema or heard about very occasionally if there was a police event on the news. Pubs were for wharfies and mates, smokers and heavy drinkers – or our neighbours down there for some liquid relief from domestic boredom.

That's the picture of growing up. Perhaps not unlike many other places in Australia and likely lots of others around the globe. Not so much inspiring as contented and comfortable. We knew little else and had no reason to feel that life should be giving us more. We accepted it for what it was and now, as I look back on it, full of good experiences mostly unrecognised then. A lesson or two thrown in. Take it all and use it for the common good – or yours!

~

My second job was as a casual in retail, a short walk from home in the local shopping centre. Saturday mornings. Then golf caddy at

Virginia, a suburb of Brisbane, for a police detective, his bag almost as heavy as he was. No such thing as golf buggies then, let alone carts. Five bob for the long afternoon and an extra shilling if he had a good round. Learning the value of work and a three-mile walk home with tired feet. Get a start somewhere, I could have thought, but back then no real idea. Normal.

A year later, also in Virginia, I played tennis on Thursday nights. Ball right into the server's corner at just under 100kph I'd like to say, but no one has a perfect memory. Not as important as those nights at the courts, my first fling with Suzie. I had a bike then and we would walk together to her home, bike alongside, for two miles in the wrong direction to say goodnight. Then I had the long ride home in the cool midnight air. A first love that crashed and burned one day when I saw her skipping down the Anzac Square steps and laughing with some other kid. She walked home from tennis alone after that and I got home earlier.

Love. Lose. Learn. Maybe that was when my journey really began. Who knows? A good way to start and just let it run, keep your balance and pick up lessons on the way.

School in later years was up on Gregory Terrace above the city, travelling home on the Kalinga tram. The line with the sharpest, most violent ninety-degree turns in the world except possibly Vienna. I'm still convinced even now the driver rammed his levers to the max going into every turn to fling the machine around at top speed, wheels lifting off the outside track, because he knew kids in the back were itching to hop off at the end to throw up. Me being first in line for that group activity.

Are we on our way yet with the list of things learned, lives lived, mission accomplished? I can give you a truckload of such things to sort through, but we haven't got time.

Then it was Brisbane Grammar further along on the Terrace and its head "Shorty" Newell, who was about nine feet tall. "Imperious Chap" on his CV, just under date and place of birth. Not too much to remember from there either. Certainly nothing to write about that might help with your own Starting Life Primer.

All I seem to go back to was helping some friends lift his Austin A30 off its wheels to place it between two palms beside the school's driveway so the front bumper touched one tree and the rear bumper touched the other. Too late to catch me now, Shorty. I think tall guys prefer tiny cars because they can do their twists and bends getting in and out without having to schedule stretching sessions for another part of their day. Two jobs at once.

Those young schooldays when someone would have an older brother with a car and we'd all drive down to Surfers Paradise on the Gold Coast for a swim and fun for the day. Big California George in the yellow Cadillac convertible on the beachfront, roof down, charming girls into buying his coconut oil. Then the long road home feeling the natural sunburn. Who needs cooking oil? Call me in thirty years and tell me about it.

A beginning

School's out! As I remember it wasn't that I longed to leave Grammar. Or that I needed to do something else. School work was all right and so was sport, but it was all just one boring week after another. Never ending. Why are we being taught all this stuff? I'd learned nothing from anybody about a world out there full of ways to do something and enjoy it. The horizon was a blank canvas that just said you work somewhere, anywhere – it doesn't matter, earn money to feed and look after yourself and go from there. Somewhere.

I was putty, as in "point me and I'll go that way." Down to parents to plot my course. The scene for lots of families then was that they couldn't really afford to carry kids, in our case three, through to university which was a whole other world quite beyond the reach of most families.

Best options for my older brother and me seemed to be a start in a bank somehow. Firm slotting into places where we wouldn't lose our jobs except by some unimaginable circumstances. Security of a known rate of pay, reliably paid weekly. A kick-off point where you could go further.

My younger sister went into nursing with some insight into wanting to do something specific, no doubt from our mother, Sister Beautiful from Tambo. But for me at least here I was. Down from Mars and unprepared in a new situation. Into the mailroom at the state office of the Bank of New South Wales at the top of Queen Street in Brisbane, waiting for someone to tell me what to do.

Things might have been similar with my brother getting into the other bank a year earlier. We never chatted about it or I would have known a bit more when my turn came. But it's about asking and listening, as I said.

A BEGINNING

The months in Brisbane passed quickly enough, mail and helping in the daily clearing house linkup with other banks before I opened a letter that said I was going to Gladstone, 500km north. The next week I was on the Sunlander long-distance train with my case of a few clothes and a second pair of shoes and on my way. Alone. At just north of sixteen years of age.

The Wales was a good employer and arranged for me to stay at Ma Lee's boarding house just a short lunchtime walk down the hill from the branch. One other bank guy was there for a while. Others were wharfies who would work in Hobart or Melbourne in summer and migrate north every winter. Good guys but smokers and drinkers – I was a lamb in a wolves' den, but they were all fine and I got into chopping the wood and mixing without trouble. At least nothing major although the tiny tattoo on my upper right arm came from a night with beers up in Auckland Park where all the young guys in town were inking up with sewing machine needles.

My first object lesson for a "bank johnny" living in a country town: don't get so far from the stream that it's hard to swim in it – hence my small diamond tattoo, self-inflicted and the minimum I felt I could get away with. That was then anyway. Pretty different now as we know.

The country life

There are two parts to this period in my career. Working in a bank. And the outside world, which was more interesting.

Inside there was always the manager and his sidekick, the accountant. They had to deal with all the serious stuff. Like keeping it all together – protecting our customer base against other predators in town, being responsible when borderline loans looked like going south, taking calls any day from one of the many who had banked with us for a hundred years and expected a nod even when anyone could see he was over-extending to pick up the acres next door for his boys or betting on a better season you knew wouldn't happen. The odd ones who maxxed out with the loan and skipped. Backing of trust and security on paper always risky and you never really know people.

The manager also had other things to ponder. How's the team coping? Is Freddy coming along, making friends over the counter with those few customers, aside from the mostly nice people, who we know go out of their way to be difficult or are just impatient or like to pick targets and come in when they know Fred's on lunchtime teller duty with his little cashbox? Who will be sent off next to another town now that things are running like clockwork? What new green kid will come on Sunday night's train to replace him? How will he settle into the room down at the pub we've fixed for him? Does he smoke? Or drink? What other stints have shaped him after he joined and started his real learning process?

There was a new area manager down in Brisbane head office. Harry was fair and a good leader, well-liked by all his branch managers. No problems any time as long as you didn't put a foot wrong. Trouble was the new guy was different and you'd heard he liked to use the whip and show everyone who's boss. Thin ice ahead. But it was what it was.

You'd been there before and seen it all in a half dozen other country branches. Part of what you signed up for.

Outside the accountant's door on the shop floor, life seemed to revolve around cheques. Millions of them in and out every day like a tide. More than all of them in the Czech Republic, we used to say.

The other thing I remember we said sometimes: if you want to get good at tennis, join a bank. Months of pulling the handle of the adding machine and your right arm was as good as that on any pro (left handers don't apply). Sort the incomings across the counter. Open the mail and sort them too. Make the piles. Commonwealth, National, ANZ. Our own belonging to a hundred other branches, some in places you'd never heard of. Others you prayed you'd never be transferred to. Use the machine, do the arm pulls and pull the printed slips to tuck under the bands of bunches of other bank cheques and so on. Move the pile of own cheques over ready for the job after lunch and all afternoon. Two jobs for the day ahead.

First, the clearing house. Always a fun hour at around eleven o'clock, meeting the others in a room down at another bank. The Commonwealth in Gladstone was where we all exchanged each other's cheques and signed for them, and I put the Wales ones they'd all given me into my bag to walk back. They were destined to go on the heap waiting for me later. We all liked each other, our little clearing house band, and I always stopped a moment to straighten my tie before going in because of the one with the sparkling eyes and the melting smile, the Commonwealth girl.

The National Bank kid was always late with his shirt half-out, last-year-of-school style. His manager knew he was a drongo but didn't stop him at the checkout gate on his way to clearing. He might snap out of it some day and besides, soon he'd be at the train station and off to the next branch as someone else's problem. Can you spot the marketing hint here? More of which will follow. Start small and destroy the bank's image bit by bit. Marketing doesn't live here. It's back in the advertising department. Who cares?

Ten minutes' work to get rid of all the other banks' cheques and collect your own, but it was always a one-hour thing just to be out and away from the grind back in the branch – same old, every day. We'd chat away, tell stories, poke fun at targets, gossip and, more often than not, pop into the milk bar before heading back along our various trails. Never any hurry-up by anyone in command. Just the way it was.

The second job of each day, the dreary one, was straight after the lunch hour spent walking down to the boarding house in Gladstone – or over to the pub where my room was in Biloela another year. The place where a stray cattle dog adopted me and always saw me as I came out of the bank for lunch, came across and lagged behind as I went down to the pub. Then waited and helped me get back to work by one thirty, before taking the afternoon off in the shade under my grey car parked outside. One afternoon everyone in the bank and half the street heard this barking and people screaming. Blue had made a mistake. It wasn't my old grey Ford. He had taken his nap under someone's grey Buick and now the owners wanted to drive home, but Blue wouldn't let them anywhere near the car doors. I never could get him to recognise brands, but a whistle and a soft word every time and it was fixed.

Me, the peacemaker. Then, if not now.

The afternoon job drifted on – for seemingly endless hours. Our own bank cheques on the branch were out of the way with the ledger keeper up on his high stool at the long sloping desk, writing up each cheque one by one into the pages of one of the four huge ledgers. Every page with an account name in about 72-point script flourish headers carefully drawn the same or better than the pages behind written with pen and ink by last year's ledger keeper. Lines, numbers, payees, amounts, balances and the red ink pen when things went out of bounds. A skill I adopted only a couple of years later, first in Oakey, in southern Queensland, I seem to remember.

The other branch cheques a daily ritual. Get the box of blank envelopes out, put them on the typewriter desk with the cheques and start. To this day I can type two lines as fast on any qwerty keyboard as any gun typist: The Manager, first line. Bank of New South Wales, second. I've typed it on millions of envelopes. Under that of course would go Cunnamulla, Geraldton, Ballarat, 260 Queen Street Brisbane or whatever for each one or sometimes a few for one bigger branch. I never understood why the printing department didn't print envelopes with "The Manager, Bank of New South Wales" and a ruled line underneath. To potentially save thousands in the cost of work hours, but maybe not because our work whatever the load always just matched the number of hours in the day. Like in Isisford where some days we would not get a single customer in the door.

Not even the publican of the only pub left in town after the other two went up in flames with a death and one pub owner locked away up in Stewart's Creek in Townsville. He forgot to throw his lighter into the bush before his turn in the police line-up.

In Blackall, as in Isisford, we were there for the wool money from Listowel Downs, Swan Hill and all the other huge holdings way out along the dirt roads – where I used to drive a truck carting the wool bales back to the railhead in shearing season as one of my other jobs, as well as writing up the monthly customer accounts at the local Greek café.

With my café job it was all about the guys down at the station waiting for the Inlander to pull in, another long-distance train, all steam and smoke, loaded up with produce to feed the shearing teams and so many others. Pencils and tear-off notepads in hand after calls from the property managers and station cooks the night before – three dozen cabbages, twelve crates of tomatoes, five dozen cartons of eggs, twenty bags of bread … endless supplies for a week. Or longer if it rained, which it wouldn't this year. For just one big station to feed fifty men or twice that and more during mustering and shearing season. More half-truckloads for dozens more big stations. Item, quantity and price per pound scribbled on every slip as it went onto the spike file and goods packed on the waiting trucks for the two hours and more drive out to station kitchens and cool sheds.

I'd get the spike files when I stepped into my little room behind the café and settle into translating the scribble and writing every station account up by hand. A few hours most days, when I got away early from the bank. No deadline. When they were done, they were done, then the Costa boys would post them out and get paid. No worries for me – hours clocked in, cash in hand from the till every Friday. And nobody over my shoulder.

The wool carrier job paid too, but that was more about the fun of learning to drive a truck. Me and Merv Williams the real truckie, also living in the Prince of Wales hotel, mates who played football together.

We would meet at Murray's truckyard late afternoon, get the two Bedfords and follow each other out of town. Across the grids, the odd dry creek bed and around the sandbogs – or mudbogs if it had rained the week before. Arrived outside the sheds about sundown where all the big bales were, rolled down the ramp as soon as the stencils dried and scattered around the derrick, wire hooked to the jeep and station hands ready.

Shearers off drinking in the quarters and comparing tallies after a long tough last day. Packing their gear for tomorrow's dusty corrugated thirty-mile main road ride and in across the grids for another mile to their next big shed, sheep waiting.

With the station hands, we spent an hour or more swinging the bales up and stacking them three high, about eighteen bales on each truck. A drink or two and we were off again, more slowly, back just before midnight at the railyards on the edge of town, two of us with just those hooks with handles for your right hand to pull the bales off and onto the flatbed carriages an inch or two beside the truck decks and up a second layer. Back in bed about two.

Bullet-proof at twenty. The only thing to watch was football every weekend, home or miles away. Always where the grass struggled as it waited for the next rain in a month or two. Skin off whenever you went down if you weren't careful in a tackle.

As good as training Thursday nights with our football gear, running around, careful our trainer Danny O'Connor, an ex-Norths player, didn't get too close with his spiky runners and put a spike through one of our football boots.

I felt I'd graduated as a truckie after a while so I walked into the police station just down from the bank.

"I'm here to get a licence," I said to the big, tough-as-nails country sergeant behind the counter.

"We've been waiting for you," he said and shoved a sheet of paper across, not unfriendly. Walked out with my new licence, no questions asked.

Years rolled happily enough onwards. New town. No new girlfriend because they were all taken. Even the ones you wouldn't walk across to the other side of the dance floor to ask if she would join you for the

THE COUNTRY LIFE

Pride of Erin. All hooked up with locals unless some guy left town. Which happened now and then.

But plenty of new friends, boys and girls. More when you got into everything going. Every sport you could handle. Join the rifle club so you could get the old .303 and buy thirty rounds that otherwise would be over your cash limit. Use fifteen on the 300- and 600-yard range and keep the others until they added up, enough to go pig shooting on a Sunday. A huge, fierce black pig tearing out of a thicket until it slowed with the dogs swinging clear in the air, hanging by their teeth, one on each ear. Other days of slow walking in 40-degree heat. Seeing fresh turned earth, but not one beast after four long hours. No sweat. Still good to be out in the gidgee scrub. Free.

Oakey, Laidley, Rockhampton, Gin Gin and other places – all good, each in its own way. People to meet and new places to explore. Ever upwards learning new tricks as in icy, pretty Killarney when the Watson boys who worked in the mill and a stock and station agent in town picked me up mid-Saturday when the bank closed to go out to the family farm in the hills. Delicious roast dinner lunch and Dad saying, "You boys might like a ride this afternoon. I've put three horses in the creek paddock. The old grey's kind and friendly for the bank johnny." You can guess where that story goes, but at least I learned to ride better.

Something everywhere. From wading in mud well above my knees in Meatworks Creek just out of Gladstone that first country year with one of those long reinforcing rods you put in a swimming pool pour, slight bend at one end. Poke it down a mudhole at low tide, twist and pull and nearly always out came a big mud crab you grabbed and threw back to a mate who threw it to Freddy still in the old boat. We rowed back across with our feet on the seats, floor crawling with monsters. Back home, Ma Lee ready with the backyard laundry copper tub boiling over the wood fire for us to throw a half dozen crabs in at a time. Heaps of so many other moments I can't ever forget.

Another springs to mind. The Bank of New South Wales Rule Book, aka the Bible. Get two copies and bits of string to tie around them. Lift one in each hand. Do that for two months and you'll be up for a spot in the next Olympics.

Maybe it's best that I don't name this next branch in case things haven't changed even now and the crims get word. You'll see what I mean in a moment.

Gerry Rodie, our rotund accountant was probably a good accountant and a nice man except for getting wasted every Friday night. I felt a bit sorry for him with his nice happy wife and kids. Family in the long paddock branch to branch for the last fifteen years.

He came out of the strongroom just after lunch one day and said, "On page 147 of the Bible it says every bank officer must undergo pistol practice twice a year. And today's the day. We leave as soon as we close the shop."

No worries for me, already an experienced shooter. From that time in Gladstone when I lived in the small bedroom at the rear of the branch to save rent while the security clerk was away. Sunday afternoons in the main street were more silent than any cemetery. Look one way. Nothing. Turn around and way down towards the creek you might catch a stray cat slinking across the drag after searching for a rat in the junk and the long weeds behind the hotel.

Under the wooden bed base I discovered a revolver hanging on a hook. Loaded. Being Sunday with not much going on, I sat on the bed and pointed it out the open window and the thing went off. Nothing happened after that despite the noise. No sirens. No windows opening in the house next door. No report to head office that would get me transferred to Julia Creek or worse, Normanton. Just the smell, but I could fix that before everyone came in the next morning.

Back to pistol practice as regulated. Gerry put two guns in coin bags, got about four cartons of shells from the top shelf in the strongroom, swept the dust off and put them in more bags and out we went. Five squeezed in his Hillman rattling along the half-mile of tar out of town and then the dirt road for another mile. We turned onto a side track and someone spotted a pitted white enamelled chamber pot already set up in the fork of a tree.

We all got out, walked over until we were about twenty metres from the target and lined up while Gerry did the loading and handed us the guns.

The chamber pot survived all the gunfire. Not even one more chip on it. That didn't mean the shooters before us were any better. Turned

THE COUNTRY LIFE

out it was the ammo that couldn't go the distance. Maximum range just under four metres and then a punch about as powerful as a spit ball. A couple of bullets I remember fell out on my shoe. I can still see Gerry now poking a pencil down the barrels to push out the spent bullets that didn't even make it out of the guns. And the odd bit of rising dust as a missile hit the dirt a few steps away. "Close range. Reload. Fire!" Same story!

"We'd better not say anything about this back at base," said Gerry on the way back. "We wouldn't want to get held up."

Who wouldn't want to have lived through those times? And all that they gave me? Even being airsick in the old DC3 flying back home to Brisbane once a year and skipping between towns all the way across the western plains never high enough to clear the hot air speedbumps. I don't mind any bit of it now. Perhaps I never did.

Big change

I got to Mackay, in north Queensland, one Sunday after my second stint in tiny Isisford. First the all-night Inlander ride to Rockhampton and up from there on the Sunlander. I'd graduated from the mailroom to general hand and ledger keeper then teller and my next step was security clerk. That was waiting for me in Mackay. Maybe. It felt good to do the switch again – from the west to the sea and sometimes back again. I settled into the place the bank had booked for me and fronted up at the branch first thing Monday.

"Don't unpack," said the manager as soon as I arrived. "You're off to the big smoke!"

Holy Cow! Sydney, New South Wales, or any place outside Queensland, was another planet for me.

While I was on my big adventure in all those great country towns, I had also seen all the other people transferring around, some often – particularly those on relieving staff which I was on for a while and earning a lot more – and others with families, rented homes and their kids being moved from school to school; married bank people seemed to be moved every three years or so. Climbing the ladder, making new friends and keeping in touch with others you'd left behind. All you signed up for. Part of the territory and hardly ever a complaint. A good secure job and a happy life with an ever-changing horizon. Something even better next year or the year after. Next shift might be back to the coast.

That was OK, but not quite for me. Would have been easy for me to stay the course and let everything unfold. Meet my life partner, have a family. All that.

But I decided to go off-road. Not knowing where it would end, but thinking if I had a skill I could try to switch if I ever felt like it without having to start another job at ground level like raking the leaves in some hotel carpark. Accountancy, no. Didn't get far last time. Selling, how to go about that from my perch? Besides that's sink or swim, unstable. Nothing involving a set goal or firm plans to leave. Rather just looking for something to help create a path into my future.

I found a way to do some study, connecting with the Institute of Sales Management and the Advertising Institute. It sounded interesting and non-clerical. I took the few books from branch to branch for a short while. Then there were exam stages to step through. No problem. I got the principal at the local school to do the honours, which involved me sitting at a classroom desk a couple of evenings while he smoked, read a book and watched the clock. He got the sealed papers one of the institutes had mailed to him at my request the week before. When I passed the odd exam I got the usual letter from the institute and showed it to the manager. In turn he sent something off to Personnel at head office.

Things were happening on the other side of the world, far from my country sphere. There was a vacancy in the Sydney head office advertising department, a department of just four, and I was the only one out of some fifteen thousand (maybe more) employees in the bank with the word "advertising" in my staff file.

After a brief stop home in Brisbane, I got to see Sydney for the first time. Room arranged in a guest house just up from the Neutral Bay ferry, where my future wife Elaine had also just moved in with her three friends after travelling in Europe for a few years. We met over breakfast one morning and I loved her friendly, bubbly nature, her ready laugh. I started taking her sailing on the harbour in a small boat I bought soon after moving to Sydney. And that was it. We were married for more than thirty wonderful years.

Advertising manager Phil Matthews welcomed me to head office and I had a front-row seat to take in everything that went on. Agencies bringing new layouts, brochures, media plans, budgets, clipping pages with our ads out of hundreds of country papers, research here and there. Bags of various promotional things for branch managers to give out, like money boxes.

Mr Matthews, as he was to me, always carried a pipe and knew it all and the bank let him ply his trade as far as I saw. Never touch "You can bank on the Wales" and the agencies knew what sort of advertising their client wanted. That's the way it was, with my contribution handling the paper stuff and doing what had to be done. No need for any creative ideas or input. All taken care of. I did what was asked and watched the steady ship sail on.

Then came the time Elaine said yes. She and her mates, all from Murwillumbah in northern NSW, had moved to Wallaringa Mansions and I shared a flat nearby looking over Mosman Bay with two others: Paul, a commercial artist, and David, an architect with a beard and an old Peugeot. Spitting image of Jesus. Very intellectual and urbane. Good culture for me. Plus Ian, an English friend of David's who turned up one day looking for a place to sleep for a few nights. Odd but harmless. I never knew what he did beyond catching seahorses while snorkelling around Clifton Gardens in Sydney Harbour when we all went to work. He was still there sleeping every night under the dining table when I moved out a year later. No worries.

Elaine and I made the decision to get married in Brisbane and relocate there. Her parents were getting on in Murwillumbah. Mine were too, in Brisbane, and the right thing to do was to see more of them while they were still around. She left her job as a photographer in a fashionable city studio and I left the Wales. No looking back. We would live at Park Hill, my family home in Brisbane, and spend as many weekends as we could down in Murwillumbah, a two-hour drive away.

No problem for Elaine getting work. But I wasn't yet set up with any sort of final qualification in advertising. Still had a couple more exam papers to go. It may not have mattered, but I didn't feel ready. So I became a door-to-door salesman of sorts, for the very old Bowkett Benefit Building Society. It had subscribers who paid a small amount into their accounts each week. A safe enough savings account with the society's offices part of a small firm of two aged accountants in the city. The interest rate was fine, matched with housing loans to members. On top was a monthly draw of an interest-free loan for one winner – as long as you remained a currently active member putting money in every week. My uncle had won once and it was a useful bonus to any lucky family at that time. I was already a member, as was my father.

I saw an opportunity. Quite a number of members had dropped off the perch as regular payers. Their account balances were intact, they were still earning interest and could withdraw anytime. But they just left it there. No more coins in the top of the money box. The society had an incentive scheme that any member getting another member to re-subscribe and start paying into his/her account regularly again would get a reward of five pounds. More paying members meant more money for monthly draws, greater accumulated funds for the accountants to make more loans and a bigger pie towards their income as a small percentage of total funds. No greed. Just cash for work done.

The incentive of five pounds per re-subscriber drew in a few renewals each month as families talked and lapsed members had a rethink. But I turned it into a job by asking if the society would pay me if I did the same, approaching everyone I could using the lapsed members list. No sweat. They were happy to let me loose. They couldn't pay any wage, but I would get the five pounds for every convert. No added cost to them, so why not?

Off I went making house calls all over Brisbane and following up. An easy sell, I thought. Not much money involved. Your old money's still there, safe as a church. Why not come back to where you left off and add to it and be in the draw for the next interest-free loan?

Within a month I was earning twice the normal wage at my level and there seemed no end to it. I had more than enough prospects to keep me going indefinitely with fresh dropouts coming onto my list all the time.

Life glided on. Never a drama. Things were good at Park Hill and we had great weekends at Elaine's family home in Murwillumbah. Tea and laughter with lovely old Mary and Ed Preston, Elaine's parents, who were loved by everyone in town. Elaine's wonderful older brothers too, all three back safe from the war and their happy families. Perfect.

One August day Reverend Pashen married us in St Stephens up on Gregory Terrace and we did the speeches at Lennons, a classy hotel in the city. Everyone was there. Off up the coast to Noosa in our VW Beetle for the honeymoon, then back home to Brisbane and a little one-and-a-half room flat at Hamilton overlooking the river. Always smooth sailing every moment, every day, for Elaine and me. Content.

Then another turn in the road. For fun we drove out to see a display home in Kenmore, the bright new Brisbane suburb just springing up. A nice, fresh, sunny, modern new home. All you'd want. A pleasant way to spend a Sunday afternoon and… we accidentally bought our first home.

The sales guy greeted us as we went in, spent half an hour showing us around, and as we went out again I asked him how much the house was.

"Six thousand, two hundred pounds," he said.

"It's really nice," I said, "but we couldn't do anything more than five thousand." As a departing friendly comment and totally off the radar of an interested offer. Definitely not for us, not yet. We had the car and no money.

Next morning he called and said the house was ours for five thousand. After we got up off the floor, we said we'd have to work something out. Please hold for a day or two. Elaine's dad gave us a thousand without blinking an eye and a few weeks later we moved in with Brandy, our new Labrador pup. New everything. A modest new start.

The advertising agency

I walked into Merchandising Publicity, an advertising agency down a side street off Fortitude Valley, just out of the Brisbane city centre. The new job was mine within half an hour. On my way up the next set of stairs. Uncertain, though, about what it was really like in "the wonderful world of advertising".

You could see it even then. Managing directors Ken Lawrence and Peg Cameron had built the agency from an empty square of land right after the war ended. The perfect advertising agency, *Truman Show*-style. Gravel space for cars and a two-level box probably drawn up by Ken himself. Reception desk and rooms on the ground floor, bright offices upstairs for themselves, a few suits, the media people and the art studio. Space for the copiers and other stuff. Kitchen at the back. Functional. Not a thing you could change.

It was successful. Respected, with a solid reputation and good clients with good advertising budgets. One could have guessed Ken was twin brother to Trevor Howard, the movie star. Same look, same almost everything, but kind enough and strong as a leader. He came out of army intelligence and obviously remained unchanged. Peg was the same. Professional, but grim. Never any fun or laughter in the house. Here are your clients, get the briefs, make up the ads and media plan, present to the client then return and execute. We had a meeting room, but I never saw it used. Clients never came. We went to them. And by the way, "Don't chat with Col, the Creative. He's working."

Col Anderson was a good mate after hours. Same age as me with a shiny green Sunbeam Alpine soft-top. But not in the office. I was creative too, with copy, but it all hung on Col's art.

I remember one day Ken called Mike Hanley, another new young suit, and me into his corner office and told us he had set us up together as "an agency within the agency". Separate books for the income from our clients' spending on production and media, less costs for a fair proportion of office overheads and of course our salaries. Each of us would get on top of a normal salary a share of the bottom line.

The intelligence officer with his new incentive plan, but for us things were looking good. And it worked well for a whole two months. Then it disappeared. No discussion. No explanation. Intelligence at its most ruthless.

Looking back, the Merchandising Publicity product was constant and predictable. Every print ad, every radio and TV commercial, fitted some sort of advertising style template, picture and words with logo at the bottom or commercial ending. Sensible, understandable and quite professional you'd have to admit. With persuasive text and slogans that would also fit the copybook. "This all fits the formula of what we in the agency know makes people want to buy!"

From my two years there I don't recall ever a moment of thrill, joy or excitement over some new advertising we had created for a client. What we did was sure to work and clients never knocked us back. They might have changed layouts or fiddled with text and fonts a bit, but they never disagreed with what the agency presented. For my clients I wrote the copy and Col did the layouts, the finished art and the storyboards. A successful place to work, but no fun or group hugs or drinks to celebrate success – or even staff meetings. This was advertising without any colour, except the yellow of our favourite client, Golden Circle.

One day I got a call from Tom Waite. He could have been taken for a cousin of that guy down at Surfers selling the Coconut Cooking Oil for beach lovers. Flashy, silk tie and shiny shoes with his agency uptown, T Hilken Waite. When he said to come and join him for almost double my current wage I talked with Elaine and decided to take Tom's offer. Ken shook my hand on the way out after a quite decent short and friendly chat. Intelligence-style. No farewell office party or drinks session. Didn't happen at good old MP, even if I had wanted it. Which I didn't. Fair enough, goodbye everyone and you too, Peg.

It was different at T Hilken Waite. Stylish. But all about the king, Tom. Our team produced advertising that met clients' expectations and Tom watched over everything with a sharp eye. His agency. His

THE ADVERTISING AGENCY

way or don't come in tomorrow. Except not much was about how exciting the ads were or brilliant thinking. More about something we all had to learn from Tom: how a world-class New York-style ad agency should conduct itself in-office and fronting clients. And underlying that were the charges to every client – media rates could be checked, but production costs were clearly sky high and no one had to know. A half-page ad in the Brisbane *Telegraph* might cost double to make up than to appear just once.

After six months or so, Elaine and I talked over dinner one evening. Very late again because of Tom's twice-weekly rantings to all staff after day's end, at times dragging on for two hours. He would give us the oil on how the agency stood at the top of the local advertising tree, how all our clients dreamed about us, how blessed we were not to be working elsewhere and so on. And on. Plus the promises at every meeting of our coming rewards like a free weekend at a top hotel in Surfers Paradise with our partners – probably including a handshake with his cousin. Never happened, as we all knew, but you couldn't not attend his meetings. Even if your granny had just gone under a bus.

I think I know now where Trump got his start in public life. The T Hilken Waite Book of Style.

Anyway, Elaine and I agreed we would sell our house in Kenmore and move to Sydney where better opportunities awaited. Next day Ed Barnum, the Australian rep for *TIME* magazine, walked into the agency on one of his regular visits from Sydney to agencies in Brisbane as in other cities. I talked with him about the advertising business and our clients and happened to mention the idea of heading south.

He called me a few days later and said if we were coming to Sydney I should go and see Ian Millar, head of McCann Erickson, global advertising agency and still a big deal today. Which I did, and got a job there as account executive on Nestle under Basil Catterns, the Kokoda hero and typical older suit in the advertising business. Elaine got a photographer job in the city the same day and the Kenmore house was sold soon after that for a good profit. We bought a block of land in Turramurra, on Sydney's leafy north shore, and built a house. Then Brandy had a litter of pups and Elaine and I had Louise, our beautiful daughter. I remember rushing home from work that day and being told by our neighbour before I left to go to the hospital, "It's a girl!"

A brave new world

My boss at McCanns, everyone's boss, was Ian Millar. Never unfriendly so much as in command, always. Take no prisoners. His efforts at humour? The Simpson Desert looked like a swamp by comparison. He knew where all the parts of the agency fit, who was the best match for each account. Which soldier might faint first. Don Drapers in every office on Level 9, one after another. The model for the *Mad Men* TV series but on a huge scale.

McCanns had come to Australia to show everyone what a real ad agency was like. Best. Brightest. Most energy. Strong. Leaders of the free world. US-style.

It was the biggest member of advertising mega-company Interpublic Group's family, top of the tree in the advertising trade around the world. McCanns owned the accounts of many of the world's top brands, acquiring more as it found weaknesses in other players and poached their accounts, rarely losing a battle.

Stars were key. In Sydney we had Bryce Courtenay. Just a year older than me, he presented like no one else. One-on-one, in any room or fronting a serious bunch of heavies in a boardroom. Always a winner. I learned a lot just watching him in action. Know your target, assemble your troops (what to say, in what order, what not to say or do, timing being critical). Then plan, don't forget drama, and execute.

I had found my place. Fingers on the top edge of the cliff ready to lift myself up onto steady ground. Where I had sort of aimed to be when I was back in the Isisford school with the principal waiting for nine o'clock to tell me to stop my exam. Not a hard climb, looking back, because I got stronger as I climbed.

With my apprenticeship under Basil on the Nestle account over, I was given the big Philips account which brought a new experience altogether. Philips' advertising manager, Bob Collins, became my new best friend.

Before Bob, Philips had had three ad managers, each of whom lasted only about six months, maybe less, and the background to that was how it all worked over there as I quickly realised. They had about fifty product managers. One for TV. One for Philishave electric razors. One for car radios. One for Infraphil lamps. One for fans and so on. And each one of them knew more about advertising than Bob, I or the whole of McCanns would ever know.

Each of the three previous guys would ply his trade and use his skillset to approve all the ads and campaign plans for every product then fill in the respective product managers. Bad idea, from the product manager's point of view. Can't have him taking control of our profit centre, our reason to exist. Get him out and let us run everything including our advertising.

Bob saw this coming clear as crystal when he took the job. From then on, every time I took anything from the agency over to Bob's office, we would make a call and drop in to the product manager's office there in the city or out in the factory to find out if the material passed muster. Nine times out of ten it would have to be changed, perhaps eleven out of ten. Copy, layout, radio or TV script, plus the media schedule, even the size of the ads which then meant new layout/copy too. You could see most of the product managers loved getting into being creative, helping with the advertising.

And back I'd come to write up the client brief on the report sheet, always on top of the material all tucked in the glossy folder that went two floors down to that other world, Creative. That was Bryce's lair where he worked with all his sycophants, creative geniuses all. You never went there to talk. Always communicated on paper – same as the fish and chips cook with his dockets in a row in the kitchen, only on a grander scale.

A month or so in, with all this going back to the client a dozen times for just one ad time after time, I made a fresh move. I wrote on my call report in the brief for Creative how I wanted the redrawn ad to look to get it over the line. Next thing, Ian calls me to come to his office.

To set this story up I should tell you my Creative on this account was Douglas X (for Xavier) Bean, a man crippled by his name as soon as he popped his head out. Best I got at school was "Sudsy" but he would have got "Lower Case X Man", held down by stature from going to capitals. He would have been fairly invisible in any room, even one filled with people of another race. Impressive to someone, but not me. So, I walked into Ian's office and there were patches of frost on his desk. The Bean sat on a side chair, mute, having done the damage. I was told in very certain terms, boldly if you like, that there was no way a Suit could ever tell a Creative how to produce an ad. Period!

I pulled down my face-shield, took a breath and said, without looking at the Bean, "Ian, do you want to create a miracle?"

He glared at me. "What?" he said.

"To get the Philips account just to break even. You can't get that by doing one ad for heaters sixteen times to get it approved, times six hundred in any given year," I said.

I knew I'd won even though I hadn't said we didn't work on billable hours and the Bean had heard, although in true MI5 style Ian couldn't bring himself to concede in any words. The five-minute meeting just ended with not much more said. I opened the door and ushered Dougie Bean out first, watching the five remaining hairs on his head until they were out of sight down the corridor to the lifts, then I walked back to my den.

Things didn't change much of course. But I was more careful poking lions after that and the Philips account hummed along notwithstanding the regular slog of present, make changes, present again, make more changes. Make the deadline, run it and get the money! Keep the account!

Like the *Mad Men* series, but long before it, we had our older grey original advertising guy from yesterday. But ours was different to Coop, the TV one.

McCann's way was to chase all their big clients around the world making sure other agencies couldn't get a foot in the door wherever possible. In Sydney they bought out Hansen and Rubensohn, another agency already well established, long before my time, and the residue was Sim Rubensohn who kept an office in the new Hansen Rubensohn McCann Erickson. Part of the deal. None of us ever saw him or his buxom sidekick with bouffant hair and nurses' heels, hand-picked by Sim and keeper of secrets from day one no doubt. They were way over

A BRAVE NEW WORLD

in the corner of my floor, Sim's office the size of a tennis court with Japanese screens, strange wall art from all over the world and antique everything to make him look rich as I saw soon enough.

Sim was probably ugly as a child. Short, cold as ice if you ever did happen to bump into him. I heard when I signed up that he was once one of the twelve faceless men of the Australian Labor Party in his younger days. I later learned to recognise the type from other encounters: gruff to perfection, manners out the window, zero listening skills, disinterested. Probably smelly if you got too close. All from the same litter – that was our Sim.

On arrival each day he used to stop his V12 Jaguar just outside, nine feet from the kerb and deaf to the honks and friendly advice from the go-arounds, and expect the driveway guy to be at attention to drive the car around the building and into the parking level at the back. Reverse that when he wanted to go home. All on phone command by the good Miss Buxom. I have no doubt the driveway guy had Sim's whip marks on his back under his shirt. How fast it went around the office one day, the day the driveway guy was quitting his job, when someone said he got the call to get the car out. As a parting gift to Sim, and having air in the basement garage, he put 120psi into all four tyres of Sim's car before he brought it around the front. Who knows where the driveway guy is now or if he even survived?

Sim's mansion was on several acres out in Dural, north-western Sydney, probably built from what he fleeced out of McCanns in the buyout. Some days you'd notice about three of the young guys missing from the mailroom if you went down there. Conscripts for the day, taken out to Dural to work in Sim's rose gardens. Probably written into the contract.

The reason people hardly ever saw him was that he had a lift key to go up and down without anyone else getting in. No mixing with us plebs, not even Ian or his seconds.

I took a call from Miss Buxom one morning to come straight away to Sim's office. She opened the door to his inner sanctum and I walked the cricket pitch-long carpet to see him, looking tiny behind his billiard table of a desk. Pens and paper, three phones and trinkets all neatly arranged. Nothing out of place. No greeting.

"Fritz Philips gave me this thing in Eindhoven in 1937," he said, waving a small radio. "Now the f---ing thing doesn't work! Get it fixed!"

He shoved it across to where I still stood to attention. If the desk hadn't been there to put me out of range, I'm sure he would have thrown it at my head and not missed.

I picked it up and crept out without a word. Back to my place in life quietly humming to myself "Evil lives amongst us".

On my next date with Bob and his masters I headed over to Philips with the precious radio in my briefcase. Bob and the radio product manager Bill Bowtell, the nicest guy and one of my best friends back then, both picked up on the situation and I left the item in their hands.

A week later Bob said it was ready and I picked it up on my next visit. They had ripped out all the insides. Diodes, transistors, wiring, maybe even crystals, and put in the chassis of a new pocket radio that was a neat fit. Then they'd joined up the volume and tuning slides at the side and the station indicator window to complete the task. A job for the most senior, most highly skilled guy on the tech team. All good. I tested it again before dropping it off with Miss Buxom. End of story. Not another word from Sim. Don Draper would have been proud of me.

Next hill

Everything was ticking along nicely. My work and place in McCanns, position in life. Elaine, tiny blonde Louise and Brandy. Our Turramurra house built, neat as new. A happy social life. Along came a new challenge. Or call it opportunity if you were looking for one, which I wasn't.

Another call to come to Ian's office.

"We opened that new office in Singapore six months ago and it has a bit of a problem," he said. "We need someone to stop it closing, get it back on its feet and make it work. You might be the man for it."

I asked him what had happened and he explained Singapore was the first of some twenty new McCann offices around the world that had started from scratch instead of buying out an established agency and its people (those worth keeping), changing from the old name and moving forward. A suitable office had been leased, six or eight staff had been put on with the first manager engaged – Soli Talyarkan, who moved across from India because his wife was a niece of the Sultan of Johor in Malaysia and wanted to be nearer to her family. I met Soli later and he was a nice man. He was put on as manager of the new office for two reasons: he was Asian and, more importantly, he had worked for J Walter Thompson in India.

Anyway, it hadn't worked out and there was much red ink. Singapore had the security of some big world brands that depended on McCanns elsewhere and automatically came over when the door opened with good local budgets and their local offices or agents in the trading houses. But it was struggling and new clients were not coming in. Soli may not have been a top salesman, but there had been worse. Notably a McCanns exec called Gregory St George Walker (GSGW) who had a long pre-opening stay in Singapore. He went everywhere, barging into the offices of all the companies he could find across town over a period of many weeks to spread the word that McCanns was the greatest, no contest. What we could do if you brought your account over to us when we opened far exceeded what you could imagine. The trouble was he didn't listen to anyone and they all saw right through him. Good manners counted in Singapore even more than in other places perhaps and I felt it soon after I settled into my new role.

GSGW had also convinced McCann World (New York) that Singapore would be in the black within twelve months of opening. I knew that wasn't going to happen, but the local Philips account would have been a big help, so I made a call and met the Singapore head of Philips, a very pleasant softly spoken Dutch man. All class. I always enjoyed chatting with him at the Tanglin Club or the Singapore Island Country Club after golf. At our first meeting he told me how much Philips Australia admired how I had dealt with them and helped them; he knew many of their product managers personally. He would have been delighted to hand me the Philips account on a silver plate knowing it would be in good hands. But it was too late. GSGW had killed any chance of that happening. The idea had been nixed back in their global head office in Eindhoven and now he couldn't even give me a chance, much as he may have wanted to.

Backing up a bit I must tell you how Ian's invitation went down. I answered his offer with a "Thanks, I'll need to talk with Elaine". Also, Singapore sounded expensive. Would we be able to afford to live there with all the usual home comforts? His response was, "I'll make sure you and Elaine will be more than satisfied."

Elaine, to her great credit and as always the perfect partner for me, said immediately that moving to Singapore was no problem and we went on discussing how it might work. Not only the house. Or what to do with Brandy. Or being away from family and friends. There was another big issue. Elaine was pregnant. Still, even that was no problem. If I had told her about a job in Argentina, she would have picked up on everything, seen it all clearly, understood and said, "When do we go?" Always capable, happy to share any heavy lifting, adding to our nest of life treasures physical and mental. Not restless, but content with what we had and if anything new came up why not have a go? I was blessed. Who could wish for more?

NEXT HILL

Moving couldn't have been easier. We gave the dog away to the neighbours ("See you when we come back, Brandy!") and found lovely tenants to care for our home.

And our new life in Singapore was great for all of us. It was hot. Every day of the year. But we got used to that in our nice breezy apartment in Hilltops, up on Cairnhill Circle. Louise ran down to the street every day to sit on the ice cream man's cart. We had a nanny/housekeeper, Lucy, to sweep, get the washing done, sweep some more and be Louise's new friend. So Elaine and I could go out most nights in every week with all the other expats. Then Tim was born, in 1967, again no dramas. That gave us another reason to move into a bigger place.

Our new home was a spacious two-storey bungalow in Bukit Timah, a residential area just north of the city centre, and we found a mother-daughter team, Fatimah and Mah Moon, to step into Lucy's shoes. Louise took up permanent residence in the wading pool on the lawn for the next year or so. Tim too, when Mah Moon let his feet touch the ground. Meanwhile Elaine and I were out somewhere every night. Friday evenings often at a big table in the Palm Court at Raffles. Dinner or just drinks at somebody's nice house. A formal casino night at the mansion of Arthur and Barbara Gough, long-time Singapore residents out from the UK years ago and never looking back. Arthur with his shaggy beard the poor man's Ernest Hemingway, we all said. Advertising Manager of *The Straits Times* for a good part of the century. Roulette wheels placed around the lighted palms in the spacious gardens and lawns, a bag of tokens as you entered, drinks at your elbow and the violins keeping up with the piano wheeled out onto the terrace.

So many memorable occasions. That was living in the tropics: you go out because it's too hot to sit home and read, watch TV or listen to music even with the aircon.

My cheeky mate Eddy Ong, advertising rep with the *Sin Chew Jit Poh* was different. Always getting me out to the seedy nightspots for a drink. More Chinese ads his way the closer we got, for sure. Lovely Chinese family at home, but a terror let loose, our Eddy.

After a while I left him to his tricks, but he still came in very handy. My office had a never-ending stream of visitors. People from all parts of the world who worked for many of our client brands came through Singapore and had to make a call on the local McCann office. Sometimes for business. More often to line me up as their guide for a night on the town. The wilder the better for many of them. No expense spared, it's a business trip! I fell for it quite a few times and nights out with a couple new mates could be good.

After a while, though, I changed all that because it just got too much. Drop by the office and we'll talk Gillette, Richardson Merrill, Goodyear, Dunlop, Agfa, Chesebrough-Ponds or whoever you are. But sorry, I have other plans tonight. I'll call my friend Eddy and he'll collect you at the hotel at six. I would then give my secretary, Alice, a hundred dollars and she'd call Soori, our messenger boy, in from his stool in the side lane and tell him to ride over and give it to Eddy at the paper. If he was busy, which was rare, he had others he could line up in a flash. Anything for McCanns, Bruce. Clockwork!

Singer was big all over the peninsula and a great client. Its local head, Fred Fairman, and his lovely wife Lucy became good friends and Fred was your typical US leader, calm but seeing all and able to make everything work. Owning a Singer, even a treadle sewing machine in the kampongs all over Malaysia was like owning cattle to the Maasai in Kenya. James Ng was sales manager and he knew the names of all seven hundred of his salespeople everywhere. As well as their wives and often the children. And how good or not so good each of those seven hundred were. He and I would spend days on the road travelling around Malaysia, group sales sessions in the afternoons and overnighting in hostels and kampong rest houses. Basic, but we had friends everywhere right up the east coast to Kota Bharu, over through the Cameron Highlands to Penang and down past Malacca.

A day flight up to the McCanns office in Kuala Lumpur happened most weeks to catch up with John Willett, technically head of both offices with me as manager of Singapore, and with Tony Eden, creative director for both offices. It was a drag taking all the ad material with me in a bag on the plane or sending it by mail. The internet would have made everything a hundred times easier.

For many clients, however, advertising was just a matter of picking up the themes and often the actual ads from the US or wherever their bigger plants were and deciding if local conversion was possible. No need to reinvent the wheel and client approval at my local end a breeze if all the parts fitted to the McCann standard. Except for translations of everything into Singapore's three other languages besides English – and the morals police.

I remember one afternoon I took a bunch of ads across town to the government department that handled approvals, necessary because the newspapers couldn't take ads without the official stamp. I got to one ad – nice picture of a couple, copy underneath, I think it was in Tamil – and the official said, "I can't approve this one."

"Why not?" I asked.

"Because I said so!" he replied.

I told him I could fix the ad if I knew how it was offending any local cultural or religious norms or customs, whatever. Our office was by necessity fully equipped with reference material if our translators ever needed to double-check anything, which was rare, and usually stuff just sailed through. All my other material for the day had been passed, but we were stuck on this last one. At last he said, "Please excuse me for a minute" and left the room. I waited, but he never came back.

Don't ask me how it ended. I don't remember, but I probably crept back to the office, binned the offending ad and fished out another one that had previously got the tick and used that instead.

~

Working on Philippine Airlines (PAL) brought lots of good experiences. McCanns had the global account so twice a year I would join all the other McCann managers with their local PAL managers from Bangkok, Hong Kong, Tokyo, Sydney, everywhere, for a conference in Manila, usually with our wives for pre-conference black tie drinks or dinner before Elaine and I spent a few days exploring the Philippines. Joe Narcisso from San Francisco, who won the PAL account for McCanns in the first place, was always there. NRMR tickets for our flights: non-revenue-must-ride.

I remember the few times when I was able to sit in the cockpit when the crew would happily show me the controls and I could watch as they brought the big jet down to land, spectacular in daylight and even more so at night. Especially in wild weather on one memorable occasion for me. Impossible to do that now, of course, but good to be in the PAL family back then.

Other things too, like nights in the plush Makati restaurants where I would see more than half the groups coming in for dinner having to check in their handguns, along with their jackets and bags. And drinks on one first evening when Lito Tionsay, very senior VP, greeted me with his ton of charm, saying, "Where's Elaine?" I told him that Singapore PAL hadn't sent a ticket over to my office for her. He spoke briefly to an aide, then turned to me saying, "She'll be here first thing in the morning." Lito was fairly typical of the Philippines elite; some in his rich family gave serious support to Marcos, I learned, whilst his brothers worked their wealth on whoever was in opposition so everyone was fine regardless of who ruled the country.

One afternoon we were all in PAL's big conference room and in walked Benigno Toda (Benny) owner of 80 per cent of the airline's stock, I was told, and clearly God to everyone. Small, pleasant, nod to all his friends, casual shirt and slacks, just a small suede zip bag on the table. Joe started up with the big presentation, all of us watching. Nothing mundane like new ads, a fresh PAL theme system-wide or TV commercials. Just the look of the planes' stripes, shapes and colours all along the fuselage and up the tail, around and under the wings. Livery it's called.

One standard PAL template and clones of that for all the fifty types of aircraft in the whole fleet, international and local and down to check-in counters, courtesy carts, tarmac vehicles – all the furniture. A full hour or longer with no questions mid-way. It all ended with one or two brief comments from the executives. Then from Benny, a thank you to Joe and he pressed the green button. The power of one. Although I expect Lito would have had to tidy up the odd wrinkle at the execution stage.

Benny rose first and smiled as he looked right around. Then everybody, upwards of about fifty in the big room, got up and drifted out. Star performance, Manila-style.

Those invited went along to the function room where our wives had gathered with other guests from the Manila business and government elite. Everyone relaxed in groups with PAL's brass wandering around to say hello to us all. An occasion because Benny was in town. Philippine hospitality on show and the business day done well with a bright new look for the planes next September.

NEXT HILL

Elaine and I were chatting with Joe and his wife Betty when Benny sauntered over, drink in one hand and his bag in the other. I noticed the bag matched his suede slacks. Cool and super rich. Benny asked Joe how long they were staying and Joe said until the weekend. This was Tuesday.

"Look," Benny said. "I'm going back to France tonight, but you can have the helicopter and pilot until you leave." He looked my way; we were in as well.

Benny loved the south of France and lived there most of every year, I'm sure just along from Monaco and his mates with boats. He might have had one too. But anyway, there we were next morning in Manila strolling out of the big hotel on Roxas Boulevard casual as you like while the silver chopper touched down on the lawn and the uniformed pilot stepped out and opened the door for us. All the American tourists packed into the breakfast room were watching as we climbed aboard, lifted off and tilted over towards Lake Taal. A moment to feel special back then when the world had a million fewer choppers tearing around. No apologies. It's a natural human thing as long as you don't get up yourself permanently.

Eighteen months on and I had moved McCanns Singapore out of our cramped, tired office (another "stroke of genius" by our GSGW at the start) and fitted out a new office with room to grow but also looking like any McCann front should look. We had collected a few more clients and were close to break-even point. However, there's one more story to tell before I wind up this chapter.

I got a call from Raffles Hotel first thing one day. It was Franz, Mr Speisshofer's assistant. They would like to visit the office this morning, ja? An hour later Gunther Speisshofer marched in, turning side-on to pass through my office doorway and still taking a bit of paint off each side. With him were two other big men who couldn't speak – at least I never found out if they could or not. One I guessed was Gunther's legal and the other probably to carry his stuff. With some quick homework I had found out Gunther was the grandson of the founder of Triumph International (underwear, not cars), based in Switzerland and huge worldwide. A McCann client in quite a few of our offices.

He was just passing through, he said, fixing new distributors in Singapore to attack this market. On to Bangkok. Then Hong Kong, and then to hook up with his film star girlfriend/fiancée in Tokyo (Akito with her own marketing plan). His mission in the visit to me was to say we could have the local account – on one condition. That we do everything sans agency commission because he was paying us everywhere else.

It was another occasion to pull down my face-shield, think and defend. There was no way I could accept this offer/demand-in-disguise. Other McCanns couldn't subsidise me and New York wouldn't throw money my way to make up the office budget. About round three across my desk, him and me with the other actors looking on, he finally settled down. He pushed his frame into a standing position, not an easy feat for someone his size, said, "OK then" and strode out, lapdogs at his heels. I'm sure he knew it wouldn't fly, but no harm in trying if you've got a few billion and aren't happy unless you get a few more. My classy Dutch friend at Philips wouldn't have gone at it that way, I thought. But we signed up with Triumph after the dust settled and it went on to be a good account.

Back home

After two and a half years my feeling was that the job was done in Singapore and to grow we needed a good Creative there. The only way for that to happen, however, was to use my salary to buy one. We already had a couple of account executives working with me to service the clients and help in producing great advertising, but to expand further we couldn't just rely on copying work from London, Brazil or anywhere else for our world brands. Mail order creative from KL was even less of a solution than it was when I'd first arrived, because of expansion.

I'm not clear if central casting got the message or not, but the stage was set. Dick Guersey, who headed McCann's big office in Manila wanted me to sit on his shoulder there, but good old Ian said he couldn't do without me back in Sydney. Besides, Elaine and I felt it would be good to move back into our Turramurra home as pre-school loomed for the two kids.

Before the pleasant sea voyage back to Australia, I was sure to pack one thing I treasured. The Christmas card that Marion Harper Jr from the top of the Interpublic tree (McCann's parent company based in New York) had sent me, which I'd framed and kept on my study wall. On the front a simple sketch of a bird and, underneath, these words, which I have passed on to so many people over so many years and which have become almost a mantra for me:

"Trust Your Hopes, Not Your Fears"

Back in Sydney I may have made things a bit hard for myself. To my obvious question first day back Ian said he would give me one of the bigger accounts. I said I'd been there, done that. Then I suggested helping as second to David Hopkins, our American McCanns rep in residence. Who knows what went into the diplomatic cables, but ostensibly he was there to pull together what offices were doing all over the world for our world brands so everyone could gain by sharing the knowledge. Commercials in Cape Town, Paris or Rio might work in Sydney or London. Get a new account in Oslo and it's a signal to chase the brand and try to sign up the account in every other place where the company operated and where we had offices.

Ian agreed and I tried pushing that envelope a bit. But it soon became clear the concept was a mirage. So I went back to a few odd clients, not so big or vital that they had to be handled by an older Don Draper, but collectively worthwhile for us to keep.

That was pretty uninspiring. I started thinking what else could I do? Then the penny dropped. Agency life was good. The thrill of being a vital cog in every client's wheel of all the things they had to get right to sell the stuff they made and pay the owners. Do your job well or the machine falls apart. Satisfying to be a part of all that.

Problem was, however, that you were always at the mercy of the guy paying the bills: the client. You see it in some movies where the agency presents the advertising and the client's people around the table love it or hate it or, worse, want to chip away and destroy it. Capable executives all, but rarely can they resist interfering (as Bryce or even the Bean used to say). Sometimes it's even positive, but they are always the bosses and don't you forget it.

Call me a control freak, but it seemed then that calling the shots when the cannon goes off would be, well, if not inspiring at least more satisfying than my work so far – now that I knew everything! At least I saw it that way in the broader marketing sense because Singapore had given me a lot of experience working with so many brands in different industries. I hadn't just been creating advertising for each client from a narrow brief. On so many occasions I had been involved in all of the client's marketing issues, plans and processes – to be sure our material fitted closely with everything else they were doing and, I should add, there were many times when my input in client meetings went well beyond making and running advertising. Not unusual in the business and perhaps even more in such places as Singapore where the local office of a big international brand would be smaller.

I decided to take my time looking around and leave when I was ready. Farewell all and to you too, Ian. Not you, Sim.

It transpired that I had three ways to go. First, the dead easy one. Get a product manager job somewhere and I'd be top dog with my own profit centre. Responsible for my own destiny and well equipped to do well with not just advertising, but everything else in the mix. Sales resources and how they were used, support right through the supply chain to the buyer, even back at square one on the board making or shipping the product and packaging it. Like Nestle's chocolate products. Or the Vaseline train at Chesebrough-Ponds. But where else before I turned onto that path?

Then a second interesting option cropped up. International financier Bernie Cornfeld was just about to set up his "Fund of Funds" operation in Australia. Managed funds were in their infancy and a whole new industry looked certain to take off (which it did) and the market was primed for a shift out of savings accounts. I followed up Bernie's ads and had a couple of chats with his henchmen. They may not have agreed, but I knew I could get it all off the ground and I saw there would have been enough money to pour into it to fuel the engines. That much from Bernie was pretty certain and he also had the templates from other countries. I was tempted to get in the ring with others wanting that exciting job. Good thing it never happened though, or I might have ended up being Bernie's cellmate, maybe not in his Swiss jail but the Queensland branch office, Boggo Road. (In 1973 Bernie Cornfeld went to prison for mismanagement of his company, Investors Overseas Services; he was acquitted in 1979. Many investors around the world lost money.)

What stopped me was an ad for Chief Marketing Manager at the good old Commercial Banking Company of Sydney. Great timing!

Stepping into marketing

The word "marketing" had been used in a general sense for ages as in "We are marketing this new type of hair oil" or "Our marketing of that rat poison has been phenomenal". Now, however, it was starting to appear in a different way.

Suddenly, in the early 1970s, it was a titled position that boards thought they had to have a box for in their company structure on page six of the annual report. Hire a marketing manager or you were so last century. You might see what I mean later.

The board of the Commercial Banking Company of Sydney (CBC) had decided the bank had to have marketing and passed the baton to the captain and he flicked it to his seconds. No point mentioning their names even though none of them is with us now. First class men clearly schooled by someone with a few clues about this brave new world in what to look for in all the candidates they could expect for the new slot. They could have seen two dozen keen applicants, asked questions, read resumes, followed up references, checked for criminal records. All that.

However, if I was one of the early birds, which I think I was, I saved them all the trouble because I held two cards: I had my banking experience *and* my experience in the outside world after I'd left the Wales. There was just one hurdle to jump over to the finish line.

"All our chief managers are in their fifties and not their early fifties," said one member of the interviewing team.

"Gentlemen," I said politely, "you may not be right on this one. Think about it. Most of your 3000 staff members are younger than you and they'll all be here when you're not. Customers in all the banks come in all sizes, but the biggest proportion of customers likely to change or be persuaded to change banks are younger than you think a chief manager must be.

STEPPING INTO MARKETING

"Who better to identify with them than me? Besides, one in every six people changes his/her bank in any year or takes up with another bank even whilst keeping ties with their old bank – that's a big target when you know nearly everyone has a bank account."

Tick. In the door at age thirty-three! Good level, money, cheap housing loan, separate management dining rooms on the top floor – morning tea up there a ritual and pick either dining room for lunch. Sometimes with the troops in the other room to be seen keeping in touch there as well as in the corridors. Driver and car outside the house in Turramurra before sunrise to get me on the first flight when I had to fly interstate. Pick my own staff, but they had to be from in the establishment. The last word on how I wanted my office to look. On and on. Might have been a bit much for some, but I could handle it.

Roger Cavan, captain at the bank, took no interest in marketing. Not his thing as I discovered during my encounter with him on my second day. The very first thing I'd been asked to do was draft a letter to go to all the staff members when they left the bank to get married, have babies or go into plumbing. Purpose being to get them to stay with the bank as customers. I did it and it came back with Roger's scrawl on the side: "What is the marketing man doing?" I still have it in a frame somewhere. That might have floored any leopard going into the jungle for the first time, but I had a bit more than average jungle experience, so I blinked twice and wandered on.

Incidentally when I left the bank ten years later and it was still kicking along, I never got my farewell letter asking me to stay on as a customer – so I missed the chance to see Roger's redraft of my perfect marketing letter. Come to think of it, I didn't get anything from the National Bank either when all the CBC customers were being moved into its marquee (National Bank and CBC merged to form the National Australia Bank in 1982). No welcome or "We aim to please". Nothing. You're ours now. Take it or leave it. We don't care either way.

A year or so after joining the CBC I reflected on that idea of marketing just being a box to tick in the company structure when I realised that in that entire year, when Roger was still in charge, I had not exchanged a single word with him. Imagine. A chief manager joining the team and not a word of welcome from its general manager let alone any enquiry into my thoughts or any discussion over a cup of tea. How far things have come! I'll say more on this in a later chapter, but you would have to wonder if the board ever asked Roger any questions about what its expensive new soldier was going to do. Clearly not. It didn't have much understanding of marketing either and, worse, wasn't interested. Roger certainly served the bank well over many preceding years, but he and the board just weren't ready for the winds of change.

Maybe that was the first moment I began having a keen eye for the quality of boards, noticing that they were good at some things, not others. I wondered how it could be that the board clearly made its decision to get marketing on the bus and two months later couldn't care less. It certainly wasn't Roger who pushed to get marketing. That was a given. Some consultant may have got to the board and it was the last agenda item of the meeting when they were all worrying about being late for lunch. Still, if the matter was looked into then surely there would have been some talk about the *function* of marketing and how it should work. I saw this later in my career: boards would deal with finance and other stuff to perfection, but were a bit lacking with marketing and needed a leg up. Sometimes.

Turns out I was the third senior appointed to the CBC since the year dot (1834, when the bank was established) after Bill Vout, our economist, and David Smith, in Computers and Systems. Everyone else was homegrown.

The marketing department numbered about seven plus a small cell in other states. These days any bank would have hundreds scattered across its empire as the marketing wing, possibly with its own HR department.

~

So if marketing was just a tick-the-box exercise, what was I there to do? Let me digress for a moment before we get to that.

Old John Maynard of Maynard Advertising, the bank's agency, was clever. Years of making ads whenever needed or a modest campaign for short periods in any year that kept people from forgetting or thinking we had closed (without exciting new themes that would have justified bigger spends and needed ongoing feeding year after year for a new image) had let him get closer to top management. Visits to the inner sanctum a few times a year, lunches with the chief at the Australian Club, Christmas cards. It all helped. The petty detail of an ad to open a branch or give Skippy the Bush Kangaroo (one of the bank's mascots) a kick along was taken care of in some department or other, but connection with the top was how to stay in business for Maynards and stitch up the money side.

Budgets were set by agreeing over tea an amount that seemed about right for who we were. No risk, no strain on the purse strings. Slight exaggeration most likely, but less science and more personal judgement. Not a big worry except it left little or no scope for a springboard into attack mode on market share. Comfortable at board level too, which brings up another interesting point.

There are so many tools like market research with all sorts of questions – brand awareness, attitudes to change, first picks, likes/dislikes, reasons for doing or not doing and a million other things – all keys to measuring how much to spend, where and on whom. All of that science is well developed to an extreme by leaders like Coca-Cola and it all goes into the mix along with ever-changing market conditions, competitor activity, history and so on. That's one side of the marketing discipline.

The other side, with tangible products at least, is material and its cost/return. Get that wrong and you pay for it. If quantities out of the factory or off the ship exceed buyer take-up, you're in trouble. Promote and sell stuff quicker than you can deliver it – trouble the other way. Goods stuck in inventory, perishables or not, and it's costly and creates more issues. All the time, competitors hovering overhead. Customers unhappy. Stockists too. Everyone you depend on.

The big difference with financial products, as I mentioned earlier in the book, is that there is no forced discipline imposed by having to deal in tangible products, inventories or distribution. It is so much harder to know when there is a perfect match between marketing effort and results. Examples are everywhere in finance. You launch a cash management trust. In comes $22 million due to two things. One: your standing in the market and any perception of product differentiation. The other: your marketing investment. If we had spent a half million less, would we have got less than the $22 million? If we had doubled the spend, would we have got $40 million? Nobody can say. Worse, same again in three months' time will be different. Same with loans. Credit cards. Everything.

We will get more if we try more – or will we? And if we do, exactly how much more will we get and did we actually spend too much? Not much different in social media marketing now even with Google rankings, clicks, the charts from Hotjar, influencers. Who knows what to expect from how many dollars spent on Google Ads targeted specifically at third generation Navajo people in certain zip codes in Western Utah or unmarried white males under fifty in some other place? You will see the clicks and that can translate into sales of products to some extent, but flow of money in financial products might be harder.

I used to say to colleagues in the trade that in financial marketing you can get away with murder compared to marketing real products (tangibles) because no one at board level demands an answer to such questions. Back then they didn't even know what questions to ask. Even if they had known, you'd have to talk them through the matter and they had little ability to present opposing views. You could claim success because some result happened. But it always will unless you really screw up. They can't sack you because you failed. Not at that anyway.

Before I go into how I made a start to help the bank move forward, a few further comments may interest you.

I often said I was an agent of change in an industry that didn't want to change. So true then but maybe not now with a bigger battlefield and the generals more mature. We learned from the last war of course. As you read this perhaps just stop and ask yourself: when was the last time your bank got in touch with you to tell you how much it valued your business or offered you some new service? The mechanism for doing so is now so much easier, but you still can't really know if they care. Same with your fund manager who sends you half-yearly reports but little else beyond the odd notice sent to everybody about some change in conditions.

Remember that thing your grandfather told you just before he left the coil? As you grow, you mature. It comes naturally, right? Otherwise, we'd all end up immature. The jury's still out on this one regarding marketing in the finance world.

It's interesting to think about *why* finance remained traditional in nature until relatively recently. Maybe it was due to depending on a few basic qualities that banks have held onto for centuries: security, dependability, reliability, even resistance to change. All seen as vital in terms of honesty and a guarantee of money remaining safe. Markets appreciated that and to some extent institutions might have felt it was enough just to maintain some brand awareness. Business grew from connections, existing customer bases and a good reputation for safety and service. Stepping out of the mainstream as a more aggressive player might have been considered risky in terms of being perceived as less safe.

So banks and other institutions ran on comfortably with staid reputations as long as they kept their books in order and complied with regulations. Was there any motivation to look at what was being done elsewhere in other industries with competitors all fighting it out for market share? Probably not.

Elsewhere I've said that tangibles have a stronger effect on boards, demanding greater constant attention to marketing than financial products because of stock. Things in packets or on showroom floors. Even cabins for ten days on a cruise or hotel room bookings. All products that have to be made available and if they're not sold there's a clear cost. With financial products you need your team to handle the work and provide a service so there is a cost. But there are no products created and left unsold if some people don't buy. The company doesn't wear a direct loss if the fund only brings in twelve million dollars not fourteen. It just misses the revenue.

Marketing equals advertising, brochures, public relations. All the trumpets. Or does it? Of course not. It may be a collective term to group all those activities together, but marketing anything, at its core, means getting everything in tune with the customer. Everybody in the business must focus on creating a perfect fit between product and user (buyer). Every tiny detail – tyre tread patterns, placement of dishwasher controls, diameter of a bottle for best fit in the hand. An endless universe that includes everything made, grown and taken out of the earth.

This is why I said to colleagues in the bank on more than one occasion, "I'm not the real chief marketing manager." I was casting a stone. "He's the one at the very top because his view goes right down to what we all do," I said. "Rates both ways, training and elevation of our people and so much more. He can bring about change far more than I can that all affects how our customers come to us, stay, and use us – and pay us."

In regional branch conferences some managers understood. Some were inspired, seeing themselves as part of the bigger picture. They would have some positive effect on their troops to help spread the culture. It was the long haul that mattered, and it did over my next ten years to a recognisable degree before the bank was swallowed by a bigger fish without mercy.

~

Back to the main song sheet. To begin, we had to do something about the bank's name. The Commercial Banking Company of Sydney. Long, offensive to people inclined to jeer across state borders for mostly no sensible reason and people mixed us up with the Commercial Bank of Australia and the Commonwealth Bank of Australia (aka CBA). Some even just called us "the Sydney"; hard to believe but I heard it myself more than once. We couldn't change the name because that was written in the Bible, but I brought it down a few syllables and simplified how we should be called: "CBC Bank". Easier in everyone's head inside the bank and, more importantly, outside. I also knew from past experience that it would grow on everyone.

Next was the awful logo past its prime. A map of Australia and the impressive fortress rising out of it at the Google location spot: Sydney. Cute, but peculiar, being kind. Imagine putting that on a flag and waving it to the people in Victoria, Queensland and Western Australia.

At McCanns we would sometimes get to see examples of old client advertising material. Not for any reason so much as something coming up in a meeting where the client felt it was relevant. When that happened, a few comments would arise about its creation. I could imagine if that had happened with the CBC's old logo, someone in the agency might have suggested its origin story went like this:

Directors around the table and from the one at the end, "Gentlemen, we have to have a logo to put over the bank's name." Then some discussion about showing the bank didn't start in Scotland or somewhere else and an office building was suggested to denote strength and the pin location to match the name.

"But Dad," said the fresh new face, two years out of Cranbrook and doing law, to the chairman, "don't you think we might one day expand into other states?"

One or two others looked up from drawing maps on their notepads and one said to another, "Make sure Tasmania is in", then they each checked their own sketches.

"Nah," said the chairman, "we might expand, but people will still be impressed that we're Australian and there's never going to be parochialism here. Everyone knows that from seeing all those other places around the world and where that got them!"

Moving forward we would be known as CBC Bank, but again it wasn't up to anyone to approve or argue the toss in any formal way. Maybe the directors woke up a year later and realised a cloud had passed over – go slowly as I said and make no noise. Best way to win. I remain thankful anyway that my immediate superiors trusted me, intentionally or not. Better than a project with a horde of experts, ten months of meetings, research and interpretation if at all useful in this instance, backwards and forwards and big dollars involved.

Now should I just put a CBC flag on top of the old fortress as the new logo? Not the answer, but to ease it off the field I had to have a replacement. The Bank of New South Wales, my old employer, had just spent close to half a million dollars on just the design (not implementation) of its new signage. Outside design specialists. Inside layers of scrutiny and evaluation right up to board level. Big deal, which I couldn't see our team was ready for. Would be more than I could manage just setting it up let alone trying to get anyone on side for the amount of money we would be spending. Not your first year in, Bruce, but find another path because it's still a first necessary step. If you don't do it, you'll be stuck with the fortress.

My design resources at Maynards didn't seem the right place to look. Or my mate Ken Elborough at Villani Art Studio who never failed to deliver exactly the look I needed for all the print, card and poster material for all our branches.

I think God sent me the answer when I spotted something in someone's sketch for the handles of the heavy doors leading into the banking chamber of a shiny new state office building we were going to impress the locals with. It had "CBC" in three squares running vertically, one letter per square, each square with cut-out corners. Turn it on its side and it worked. Tried it in our next print ads. Still good. Go further with brochures and counter cards. Still good, but no comment from upstairs. Get ahead if you make no noise, I remembered.

Next natural step was outside signage for all the branches and choosing the right colours, avoiding not only other banks' colours but things like green trees and blue sky behind the signs in hundreds of our country branches. Then the same colour would need to be used in all our other material for a uniform corporate identity.

I had done some study years before with Louis Cheskin of the Colour Research Institute in Chicago who proved that the same washing powder in three separate packets – one blue, one yellow and one a combination of blue and yellow – produced different washing results. Blue didn't get all the dirt out. Yellow destroyed the fabrics. But the blue/yellow worked fine.

From that, as simple explanation, how people feel and react to different colours also depends on what you're selling. I cast the die working late in the office one night. A distinctive orange that had to be a particular Pantone colour so it could be specified and used correctly without variation by printers and all other suppliers. Some careful consideration and I moved forward with it. Ken, back at Villanis, did a superb job with a formal corporate identity manual for all our outside suppliers and the printing department at nominal cost that wouldn't have raised eyebrows. Properties department had to progressively do new branch signage work. There had to be new cheque books. New deposit slips. New letterheads. Everything; in some cases sensibly winding down old stock to limit wastage. I recall British Paints made their own version of my standard Pantone colour, calling it Monkey Blood Pink.

The story goes on. The CBC made its own stronger footprint in the market as it grew and changed. I visited, looked and talked with banks overseas and one time brought back the simple thing of one single queue, instead of multiple lines, which we introduced first in Double Bay in Sydney; the Wales followed suit in one of their branches two weeks later. People everywhere disliked standing in the "wrong" queue, no matter where they were. Not just in banks. Soon everyone picked up on single lines leading to multiple service counters. I claim it as a first because I pushed the idea after chatting with people happy enough in long single bank queues in California and it was simple to adopt.

To use what skills you have, look for opportunities and be an agent of change brings its own satisfaction.

~

Further opportunity came with banks in Australia first issuing credit cards. When it did happen some dogs and cats got their own cards at the launch – because of odd cases where customers kept bank accounts in the names of their pets. Strange, but true. Besides the cards in some cases might have been better in their hands (paws).

American Express (Amex), Visa and Mastercard had been urging the banks for years to bring out a card. I don't know why they never succeeded. It could have been down to who got how much out of it. Anyway, one day a report sailed through my office to be read and passed on to other chiefs. It was about the banks doing their own card thing, collectively. The possible names page caught my eye and I scribbled something on the side, not too boldly to raise hackles anywhere, but enough to get attention. Then I sent it on. A few days later Geoffrey Bowen, who had succeeded Roger at the helm, stopped me in the corridor.

"How strongly do you feel about what you wrote about the new card name?" he said. I asked why and he said all the bank bosses were to meet next day and were lined up to call it Advantage (I think it was) because of a UK success and because J Walter Thompson had strongly recommended it – and they were the experts.

I told him, politely, to take a half-brick into the big meeting and threaten all who voted *not* to call it Bankcard – because of public worry about credit card costs and the fact that banks at least were trusted, if not universally liked. Off he walked. No follow up meeting of the brass to consolidate our position or have the seniors express and hear views around the table for consensus.

Next day he called and said, "Congratulations. The name's Bankcard." Another job done. Agent of change in the establishment. Tick!

One of my filing cabinets was called The Bazaar. I loved all the branch managers like brothers and from my own country experience I knew what their lives were like out in the field. They and their platoons were the front line holding our ground and winning some from the enemy, as in all wars (at least up until then). I was in the position of being able to provide one type of ammunition – little things with a smile to help make customers like us. Not toasters and hair dryers like US bank rewards, but stuff everybody could use without crippling costs.

The Bazaar contained folders on all sorts of items that suppliers offered us, with quotes per 100 or 1000 delivered in bags of fifty. Some samples in the bottom drawer. We got proposals every second day by mail or in person. Or via my marketing staff in other states. The thing was picking the ones that worked. Something practical that would be kept and reused, like golf markers. Or things to take home like metric conversion slide cards. All branded CBC Bank in Monkey Blood Pink. Nothing cheap and nasty. And hand them out judiciously. Steady flow throughout the year so the troops wouldn't hold and spend all their ammunition at once.

Managers welcomed our support too. And created opportunities. Kiama on the NSW south coast with lots of trawler customers wanted something to throw in for the annual Blessing of the Fleet festival. Cash? Donation to charity? I could do better than that. It took weeks to find someone to make up a small pewter lighthouse with base and plaque for the branch manager to give to the winner of the best decorated trawler. His small speech handing it over in front of thousands on Easter Sunday was worth the effort. But the picture in the *Mercury* next day with our manager being sure to hold the trophy with plaque at front presenting to the winner with the mayor on the other side and three lines below – that was worth more than six weeks of paid advertising considering it also might reach a couple other local rags.

The marketing angle easily missed in this small story is that sponsors like the bank would get some credit with some in an audience for doing something special rather than just handing over the usual giant-sized cheque as a donation. Little things to support our image.

Donation requests from everywhere used to gravitate to marketing. You couldn't ignore where customers were good value and had been with us for a century or much less, but all were valuable customers if they'd spent time in our shed. They all counted. We happily gave to the Society for Crippled Children, as it was known then. And many others including the Royal Institute for Deaf and Blind Children where I also picked up the job as one of three judges for the annual Lovely Motherhood Quest – a not unpleasant full Saturday each year that Elaine called a "fringe benefit" as she ironed my shirt before I got in the car to leave. Not a day to look shabby for all the pretty ladies!

La Fiamma, an Italian community newspaper and our good friends for thirty years, looked on shaky ground one time according to our Newtown branch in Sydney. Helping them without feeling I misused part of my budget (if I had one, which I didn't) was simple. Told Maynards to double up on the normal quarter page ads for a while. Justified with our strong position in the Italian community.

Customers often got to know which branch manager was a softer target than others to hit up for a questionable loan in those days. Now it's thirteen forms to fill out and your driver's licence. They also knew their bank could be approachable for something extra sometimes – we give you our business so why not give us something back?

This fell into view one day with Sydney's Taronga Zoo. Substantial customers for fifty years with funds flowing in every six months from the government as half of the Zoo's budget against operating expenses, the other half expected from gate takings every day except Christmas Day. Things were a little tight, so the Zoo chairman decided best way out was to put the squeeze on all the Zoo's suppliers and connections.

The letter to the bank as one of those suppliers came to me. I felt we couldn't make a donation of the size they would expect since they didn't have to look after people who survive on charity. But we couldn't turn them down either. So I called 2CH and arranged for radio spots every Saturday morning called "What's new at the Zoo – brought to you by CBC Bank". I asked my secretary Frances to call the garage and Tom, one of the bank's drivers, came around to Hunter Street, in the city centre, in a white car to take me over the bridge to the chairman's office in his architects' firm at Cremorne on the north side of Sydney Harbour. I didn't use bank cars or drivers from our small fleet too often, but that was an occasion for such a visit to be taken more seriously, to get the job done.

I told the chairman he didn't have a money problem; he had a marketing problem.

"Families visit the Zoo on average once in every three years," I said. "If we can help you get that up to visiting once every eighteen months or more that will fix it and the way to do that is to capture a good slice of all the families not already committed to weekend plans. Reminders every ten minutes at the right time on Saturday mornings. Use the levers of a newborn tiger or whatever to get the kids to pressure Mum and all you have to do is have someone at the Zoo take a call from 2CH late Friday each week and tell the station what new animals have been born or have arrived. The cuter and cuddlier the better."

The next week "What's new at the Zoo" launched. The following week the Zoo had a new marketing committee: me plus a couple of others from inside the Zoo and outside. Another win all round.

As the weeks rolled on it became clear we had helped: the weekend takings were getting better. Then at one meeting I suggested starting "Twilight at the Zoo" events. A perfect time to see the animals, some getting ready for bed, others doing their stretches for a wild night out. The jungle comes alive after dark, I thought. Anyone who has ever slept in a tent knows that.

Of course, it was a lead balloon. Staff wouldn't wear the roster. Impossible to work out staff rates. Besides, no-one wanted to go to the Zoo at dinnertime. Establishment: one. Agent of change: zero. A few years later and there it was – "Twilight at Taronga" up in lights, a new nocturnal experience – and everyone loved it. But I was long gone.

I should add a bit more to this. With my honorary marketing committee cap needing a wash after a year's wear, I was asked if I would accept an invitation to join the board of the Zoo. It would be an honour, I said, as long as my employer was OK with it. No money. Just my name in the annual report. I already had the free family pass including entry to Dubbo's Western Plains Zoo, north-west of Sydney, which I had a small part in opening. The Premier at the time had balked at getting in the charter plane for the short flight to Dubbo and told his Minister to step aboard instead. If Australia wasn't ready for an open-range zoo, he figured, it wasn't him wasting taxpayers' money. And if it worked, he could take full credit. It did work and I saw later that he did take credit. Dubbo became a success, but I didn't look back.

A month after the chat about joining the board Elaine and I went to the Zoo's 50th Anniversary Dinner. Formal gear, mingled a while until this dumpy Eddy lookalike sidled over, introduced himself and after the perfunctory chat said, "And what political party do you support, Bruce?" Straight out, no subtlety. I said something like I was agnostic and looked at the policies everyone put out. Hitman's mission done for the night, off he went to harass someone else.

I thought of him and Sim as from the same litter, but knew what would happen next. Or wouldn't happen. Sure enough, not another word about the Zoo board, although our committee ran on. No worries. No loss for me; it might have led to other things but I didn't need it. I had more than enough to feel satisfied and I had learned at birth never to be driven by ego.

Looking back, I feel that talk with the Zoo chairman may have put Taronga Zoo on track to develop a marketing culture. Until then the Zoo had progressed well beyond the old days of cages for almost all its residents and it was popular, but that progress may have been more about improving the welfare of the animals. Quickly forming a marketing committee and then that idea of a board slot, even if it was killed off by Sim's mates, seems to suggest that this agent of change had some lasting effect.

~

Some more stories from my CBC days. The first is about advertising.

Lyle Schwarz and his young team at Maynards remained good partners with me and while old John was off somewhere else, we all knew our trade and how to ply it. The bank became a noticeable advertiser and jackals constantly prowled for the account, mostly full of Beans who knew it all. There were uninvited submissions for the account, pretty much all wanting us to send Skippy back to the bush, scrap the Money Managers advertising theme we had started to develop and build on, and bring in a green frog or happy snaps of people jumping out of planes or something. Anything to attract attention, but not as extreme as John Singleton smashing food with a mallet in some famous TV ads that aired a few years earlier.

Research showed no worrying problems and positive value for what I spent. We had clearly emerged with a stronger identity appropriate to our business with no serious reasons to switch tack. Talk to the market the same way as over the counter. Stay on message and let it build. In my case using the Money Managers theme consistently. Don't promise what you can't deliver. Don't annoy customers or think you'll get and keep their attention with fireworks and empty appeals. Be relevant but imaginative where that fits. Be distinctive and separate from the others. All that and more, a good Creative might say.

Customers should be able to trust their bank. Always best to look like they can. Big green frogs and all-yellow parachutists in a daisy chain, we don't need you.

Our glorious place for training managers and accountants, Fernleigh Castle in Double Bay, was a grand place to go for the Friday night closing dinners for every course of twenty new trainees. Stirring speeches and people ready for the next leap in their illustrious careers. The port decanters (no bottles in that proud setting) getting giddy going so many times around the big table. Students were getting younger before my eyes because of our rate of new branch openings.

I used to tell John Gibson, who was responsible for finding the right places for new branches and worked in a little offshoot of my part of the bank, two things whenever he went off on one of his missions. Wear your fishing clothes and do a deal with the airport rental guy for the car with the scratches down both sides and a dent in the rear bumper too (if available or put one in). Pay the premium rate, but don't pick the shiniest car. John was up for this because he had many raids over foreign countries under his belt already.

I also encouraged him to bring back his suggestions for seven locations we should open next in, say, Western Australia because then we might get three. If he brought back three, we would get one, maybe two. The fishing gear and the rental car was about not getting fleeced on the real estate of course.

Our new recruits didn't go into new branches, of course. They went into the system, but soon enough through the ever-moving process of shuffling people around (for their own good) we had our youngest ever branch manager, a 28-year-old woman. A few more years on this track and we might have had a new branch manager taking up his or her appointment on the same day he or she celebrated their twenty-first birthday.

Why do I insert this story? Because it's one thing for the board to define a course of expansion, but marketing comes into the frame in execution along with finance, personnel and all the other team members. A marketing approach clearly made some contribution back then in designing new branch buildings to look more welcoming than the brick bastions of our long-established competitors in many towns and suburbs.

Our CBC was the small kid in the gang of five or so banks in Australia at the time. We opened more than 200 new branches in my ten years there, but still the other banks were taller, some noisier.

Still, I had done the maths and put us at number 138 in the free world of more than 38,000 banks. Not to be sneezed at when I attended a conference of the American Bank Marketing Association in Los Angeles one year. A thousand people there at the talkfest and you could spot the guys from Idaho or Iowa who owned their own banks. I didn't feel like a minnow in the pond at all. A lot of good speeches over those three days. Others would have put a kelpie to sleep. It didn't seem that US banks were doing things much differently to us, aside from the wide use of giveaway items to attract new customers, but there was a lot of useful conversation. One small story from that conference might amuse you.

As the huge closing dinner finished and everyone was shuffling out, I heard this loud southern drawl right behind my ear. Hank, President, First National Bank of Montana I think was on his tag.

"Hey, buddy! I'll give you a hundred bucks for your tie!" he drawled.

I politely told him it wasn't for sale. Imagine him at his loud dinner parties back home wearing my platypus tie! No way. My bank wasn't for sale and neither was I. Note: back then it was de rigueur for Aussies to travel wearing a kangaroo tie or lapel pin; my platypus tie from the Zoo served the same purpose. Now the terrorists don't care where you're from.

~

The media in Australia always treated me well as long as I had advertising dollars in my pocket to spend. I also may have been seen as having some influence being honorary treasurer of the Australian Association of National Advertisers (AANA). Elaine and I had front row seats at the tennis and other major events, but favours handed out could sometimes mean favours expected.

Committees here and there were all part of the scene, but one stood out. I was asked and agreed to fill a slot on the Advertising Standards Authority, the pre-cursor to the current regulator with the clout of a Canberra connection in the form of Sir Richard Kirby, mate of Federal politician (and soon to be Prime Minister) Bob Hawke, as chairman.

Our five members met about every quarter in one or other of the capital cities to pass judgement on public complaints and act on them when appropriate. Cases of agencies and their clients running wild to get attention and media taking the money with material that might be going too far. Not strictly Presbyterian but working to standards of common decency and an AANA code of ethics and giving the Minister scope to get involved where the Authority's efforts brought little result. All worth doing, but no doubt a much greater challenge today with the huge influence of social media.

My biggest take from all that was the experience of working with Sir Richard. He had retired as head of the Arbitration Commission and was still in touch with so many, as I saw wherever our meetings were held and he would have others join us for lunch or drinks.

He was old even then and not in the best of health. Walked with a stick, but left his home down at Cudmirrah, just south of Sydney, to drive up to the city and overnight there to catch the first flight out next morning to wherever our next meeting was. Handled every meeting well and never missed a beat in leading the panel debate on anything, despite never having worked in advertising. You just have to admire great people like him choosing not to read a book in the sun down at the beach house, but to do a bit more for Australia regardless of serious handicap. What an effort. One of my heroes forever.

Exploring

This story might add a few more pages to the book, but I think it's worth telling about my first trip overseas with the CBC Bank.

Roger, my beloved first grand master at the bank, had moved off to his retirement home not soon enough in my view and was replaced by Geoffrey Bowen. Vastly better equipped with a functioning brain to deal with a marketing type like me. Sir Geoffrey Bowen he became later, after I left the bank. I greatly admired him then and still do.

Geoffrey stopped me in the corridor one day. Our way of meeting every now and then to agree on a few odd things without subordinates making them messy with personal opinions. Couldn't happen anywhere now with formality and procedures clamped down tight on every company group discussion. Some places today might even have phone tapping.

Anyway, in our 45-second corridor conference Geoffrey said I might like to look at some banks around the world, so off you go, but pick a travel buddy you want to go with. Apparently one of our chiefs had stepped out of the trenches and wandered off on his own a few years before I arrived at the CBC and had died during a round of visits to banks in Tokyo, leading to a host of complications that followed.

I took a week or so to make up my travel map and at the same time looked around for who should come for the ride. It was clear I could pick any one of a dozen wonderful companions whose status justified their ticket and whose company I would enjoy on our journey of four weeks or so. Yet there was this other new chief, let's call him Tony, who I saw as worth the bank's investment in our not inexpensive trip – first class and six-star everything as befitted CBC ambassadors if anyone spotted us.

I had seen Tony's somewhat meteoric rise through a couple of levels and it was clear he was destined to go further. So being the responsible executive I settled my mind on him and did my mapping. Up until then it was Geoffrey's and my little secret. I didn't tell Tony at that stage of course.

Next step was to tell my immediate boss, Norm Winckle, with whom I had a more or less formal meeting each Tuesday so I could tell him where I had wasted the bank's money the week before and give him a heads up on a few highlights. To everyone in the bank he was one of those people you had to love. Clear, forthright, impatient with fools, but so engaging he could melt Joe Stalin, any occasion. Everywhere we went.

Norm had no problem putting aside instantly that Geoffrey had gone behind his back to get my trip underway and was delighted it was happening. But when I told him I had decided on Tony he exploded. "Why would you want to take that shit with you?" he said. His exact words.

Taking Tony with me was the right executive move and he was obviously seen for his ability to make decisions and sort through all the usual chaff. I had sat with him often in the seniors dining room, at state functions and regional conferences to see what he would be like as a travelling companion. As it turned out he took my news of the trip with, I thought, a shade less enthusiasm than I felt. Positive, but I imagined with a far shorter list of things he wanted to check out than my own list. But then, I was the agent of change.

He was pleasant enough to talk with in cabs and over breakfast or wandering around, but he had a couple of habits as I remember: constantly moving the salt and pepper shakers around the table at every meal and throwing tantrums in every city. San Francisco, New York, Chicago, Las Vegas, Acapulco. Yes, I did slide in a few stops that suited me and I was ready with the name of the Acapulco bank if anyone asked to see our itinerary. But nobody did. Just go, learn, come back and try things, and don't disturb us too much.

So off we went. Cities in the US and Canada and across the world: Mexico City, Moscow, London. Everywhere it was a battle about when we had to leave for the airport – four or five hours prior to departure was his choice. Mine somewhat less, so that our 28-day sojourn wouldn't be whittled down to 23 days plus cumulative time at airports. We still went to the airport together each time so I guess I won and, wary of where he might go in the bank structure by next Easter, I

EXPLORING

was always diplomatic enough during our slight confrontations to not remind him that it was my trip and I had favoured him with a free pass. Don't poke the lions, I remembered. Even sleeping ones.

As senior representatives of a major bank on the world scale it was easy to set up visits with lots of the overseas banks and discussions were fruitful all round, comparing and learning. I didn't see anywhere that other places were much ahead of where we were in the broader sense of marketing in their banks or ours – marketing was still a new weapon in the finance world. Although some were leap years ahead in things like those free toasters for new customers.

One thing I particularly enjoyed about the arranged meet-and-greets, apart from the office meetings with various executives in the banks we visited, were the lunches. No booked tables at fancy restaurants. Everything was in-house.

CBC guests today in Dining Room Three often with menus showing our bank name, logo and our names/titles (to help the handpicked bunch of hosts remember our names, I realised later) and waiters behind chairs. Citibank, Chase, Wells Fargo, Standard Chartered, Mellon and others, everywhere. Business talk and shared laughter along with the class and quality of everything. My mate held off from rearranging the salt and pepper shakers. I glared across at him once and he must have got the message. He could hold his own though in all the moments we met with others as an experienced senior banker, so that was all fine.

Geoffrey had said before we left not to write up reports. His class again. But we still did during our stopover in Tahiti. Maybe now there would be at least sixty pages to send around for everyone to read, comments added in margins and the basis for group meetings. More work for supervisors to justify their roles and report up the line.

In my planning for the stop in Mexico City I had decided to use the Singapore Visitors Guidebook and set up a local I knew to meet and look after us, aside from a couple of local bank engagements. Danny Martinez had gouged some money out of the CBC by getting us to buy very expensive pages in his publication, *The International Auge de Mexico – Australia*. A glossy coffee-table publication, prestige all the way. Editions every year in many countries. Germany, Sweden, Israel. An endless list.

Neat. And my friend Danny could play it well. Pick any country, go there, grab some editorial on the economy, tourism, history and pick up a few interviews for content. Then catch the fish. Circulation not that huge but read by all the titans. Most likely waiting for their weekly hair trims. Or the secretaries on their bus rides home. His mode of operation was to make an appointment with a CEO, become friendly and bring out the latest issue on Switzerland. Then convince his target that not being a part of such a prominent publication seen by everyone who ever went or wanted to go to and be seen at Davos when BHP and lots of others were in would be a mistake. Then he would get to see me, but of course I was locked in for the money by then. And you couldn't just say it was not cheap – it was off the scale.

There were a few other occasions in my ten years when things came up which were a choice between pleasing the boss or doing my job. That magazine page was one to let go, but I generally took pride in not flinching in the face of such challenges even though a couple of times it put me offside for a day or two until other parties got past their emotional thought processes. Living with yourself comes first. I never told them how to lend money even though on those odd occasions they knew better than I did how to do my job. Maybe.

Anyway, since I had chosen not to argue the toss over the *International Auge de Mexico – Australia* back the year before, that meant I could use Danny.

He picked us up at the airport in what he said then was the only Lamborghini in all of Mexico, cartels preferring Beechcrafts, and we had the slowest ride to his hotel – thanks to having to slow down to 5kph at every dip in the road. The hotel was a U-shaped two-storey affair, the usual colonnade style, but not what we had become used to by then. I could see if he cranked up his global trips a bit per year, he'd be on his way to a second crappy hotel pretty soon. Not hard to see he was no slouch, probably smart enough to con even Gunther for Triumph ads in editions for sixteen or more countries where Triumph garments graced the salons.

Tony and I both agreed for once that actually we didn't need Danny to show us around and went our own way from there. Besides, it would have worked against me when he came around for a chat with Geoffrey again the next year. I never told Geoffrey in our corridor meetups that I had caught up with Danny over in Mexico City, but it would have got into his kit of tricks for sure if we had used more of his hospitality. Interesting enough as a tourist city and plenty to see and do with things like the night visit out to the floodlit ruins.

One small story to tell you before we end this chapter. Tony and I had each bought some of that colourful Mexican fabric for our wives. Different patterns might have been better, but they were exactly the same and after getting home Elaine and Jean, Tony's wife, had put them to good use. When the Annual CBC Staff Ball came around a few weeks later, you guessed it, Elaine and Jean were both wearing identical skirts in the same Mexican colours and patterns trying not to look embarrassed. I think about that whenever I see our PM in a photoshoot with other leaders somewhere in the world, all in local shirts.

Next match

Eventually it became time to look over the fence. I started to feel I had done the job I needed to do at the bank and someone else could take it forward from there. One day a consultant I knew called me to ask how to get in the door to see Chris Fletcher, head of our finance arm, known as CAGA. I told him how to handle it and he said by the way Perpetual Trustees is looking around for a marketing man. No straight lines for consultants!

To my hesitant nod he set up a morning tea with John Sanders, the very likeable and capable chief executive at Perpetual Trustees. In our conversation I put my cards on the table – happy to help, but you must be committed to some hard changes if you are really serious about marketing. He promised me that the group was, and I settled the deal the following week when the chairman joined us and made the same commitment. I also felt comfortable making the change since I had seen their advertisement seeking a marketing head. I therefore assumed that they had a clear enough vision of the direction they wanted to go, considering that the financial world had advanced since I had started with the bank ten years earlier. Hopefully they had a greater appreciation of marketing.

As it turned out it was another case of getting a marketing box in the structure chart with all the passport photos of the senior executive team on a page in the annual report because it was the thing to do. This next chapter might therefore be a short one. Let's see what stories emerge.

First things first, I created a fresh logo – to represent money and the solid combination of all four of our state companies in the group – at some serious expense and with top professional help. It was accepted without much debate, but then some directors made jokes about it. Not a good sign in terms of who might see why I was on the team and who didn't have a clue.

NEXT MATCH

The road was a bit rocky from the start. They were all friendly people in Sydney and the same whenever I visited the companies in other states, but they each appeared independent in spirit and none seemed much interested or ready to hear about changes I might propose as I moved into my new role. Obviously comfortable businesses in each state, but giving clear signs that the idea of bringing some marketing talent into the group had not been sold to them.

As you might expect in Queensland, Brian Ball, Perpetual's head there, wasn't going to let even God change his name from Queensland Trustees to something with Perpetual in it and the board had little ability, and even less interest, in seeking my opinion to work out the other side of that debate to arrive at a reasonable conclusion. Leave things as they are. We're all doing well and in good shape, no sense rocking the boat. This agent of change was in the wrong paddock.

Anyway, as you now know I was used to playing a long game. A committed optimist, you might say. My small marketing team included one or two in each capital city and together we moved along with polishing the group's identity and useful media efforts. "Forged ahead" wouldn't be the right words, but we made good old Perpetual look less like it still belonged in the previous century. Not that I had cause to be critical. It was a sound business in all respects and extremely capable of providing consistent, adequate returns for the owners, beating off the enemy and standing tall in the community. It did many things well, but as time went on a missing jigsaw piece seemed to emerge.

We expected natural growth and that would happen as it always did. However, the whole world of money was picking up speed. Perpetual was happy taking a share of business that came its way, but the team found it hard to recognise that it also had the ability to gear up to get the best out of growing opportunities. I couldn't quite get it out of its comfort zone.

One can be critical of others, but the issue deserves more serious thought. Basically, I believe it all came down to the culture of the organisation: it had become accustomed to a comfortable existence over decades with virtually no pressure to make fundamental changes. Looking back this was evident at both levels, the executive and the board. Levels of business in both corporate trust and personal trust were reliable year after year, with trusteeships assured to stretch way into the future and the security of large numbers of wills held and likely to only increase as time went on. Also, ongoing estates and an established base of investing clients comfortable with common funds' performance and Perpetual's perceived security.

We also had certain insurance that helped to balance out reported profits year on year with income put aside as "reserved corpus commission" in any particular year when it suited us. To explain, an accepted practice of trust organisations is to take "corpus commission" on estate value into their accounts in two ways – as revenue in the current year on the basis of estates being settled and all distributions made in that year and, on the other hand, to put aside some revenue taken from estates as "reserved corpus commission" against work required in future on those estates having more lasting provisions for beneficiaries, such as until some reached adult age. This useful repository allowed for accounts to be topped up in any tougher year to produce fairly even group profit results year on year. That comfort level in Perpetual in my view meant we felt less need to become more aggressive in the marketplace – coupled with some limitations on understanding the real scope and potential of positive marketing, including where and how it could be used beyond the more visible elements of simple promotion and branding.

Bernie's Fund of Funds might have faded in Australia, but new managed funds began springing up everywhere like weeds. Every managed fund is governed by a set of rules known as a trust deed setting out your rights and its powers. We got more than our fair share of the trusteeships of funds coming on stream partly because Perpetual was strong, stable and experienced – having started in Australia in 1886 – and to Perpetual's credit we did do a good job in that market going at every target that popped up or was certain to be next out. First cash management trust by AFT or Macquarie, others by AMP, MLC and new investment houses springing up everywhere with new products. Each one had to have a trustee in the trust deed.

Meanwhile all our common funds were ticking along. Keeping performance mid-range with their portfolios in tune with markets so none of the beneficiaries got too upset. There my marketing contribution was to make the printed annual reports on the funds look pretty – no bland plain wrappers. Perpetual's common funds were on the same playing field as all the new managed funds, but nobody wanted to pick up the ball in terms of seeking new money by competing in the rapidly expanding wider market. The common funds existed for all our deceased estates and beneficiaries, not all the people out there suddenly seeing new ways to invest.

In a few meetings there were discussions about measuring the performance of our funds against all or some of those managed funds coming on stream and telling the public about it, but that was left on the shelf. A bit new for Perpetual to get into the wider market that way, some felt. They also had reservations that going public on fund performance in one half-year may turn into a stone around our necks next half in the event of a downturn.

As I recall however, the bigger problem was that we would be competing with the managed funds run by our corporate trust clients with whom we had trust deeds. I was the sole advocate in our executive committee for moving in such a direction and because of no positive resolve around the table it had zero chance of getting past and up for further discussion at board level.

This example leads into the wider perspective of how directors on finance boards miss out on opportunities to develop their views towards constructive marketing. They have no chance when they are not involved and of course there was no scope for me to break from our team to have my own discussion with a director at any opportune time. That rarely works.

We had our funds and wide connections with people happy to keep some of their money with us. Many were estate beneficiaries from years ago still used to having their money safe with someone they knew. I remember talking with one lady who had been with us for many years. She had just received our annual funds report, but had to admit she had no idea which of our common funds held her money. Just content to trust us. We had limited contact with clients beyond issuing standard forms of advice on their investments or an estate matter, unless clients called with questions.

All the managed funds outside were hard at it, enlisting agents everywhere they could, and all they had to do was not screw up with investment strategy, give the agents constant updates on earnings and keep the fees as quiet as possible. And pay commission on new money and money held – ongoing commission. Not new or rocket science. Perpetual wasn't interested in paying anybody any commission. The root cause of missing that one. We'll just do our own thing as always.

I visited Paul Terry, at that time head of Monitor Money, a huge investment house, in his luxurious office on Sydney's north shore one afternoon to try to get him to include Perpetual funds in the mix with millions flowing into funds under his control each fortnight from the pay packets of all the armed forces people nationwide. My suggestion was that including Perpetual in the list of where clients' money was safely tucked away, a vast amount all up, would have given his whole shopfront added stature. But he didn't take the bait and I might have known it was a losing proposition in the first place. No commission, no sale. Still, we had a very pleasant hour or two and I felt sad years later when I heard that Paul had been killed on his first solo helicopter flight, in Hawaii.

Our business kept healthy with the two trust sides, personal and corporate, corpus commission and fees on every dollar, as normal. Besides the estates, some beneficiaries settling and out the door with cash distributed and some staying under will provisions, there were lots of people putting money with us from earlier connections and a few window shoppers, all adding up to millions – funds under management (FUM).

But it was no use trying to get our guys excited about the obvious potential or running onto the field against the outside managed funds industry. Marketing couldn't tell them how to do their jobs.

I had brought back from a trust conference in the US a couple of ideas. One, that some trust companies in America were gearing up to get the super-rich as prime clients. Huge dollars. It seemed that many liked having a one-stop shop to do everything for them, money-wise, while they focussed on changing the world. More convenient than having legal help on one side of town, investment on another, tax and accounting elsewhere, with coordination depending on their right-hand men putting it all together. Some trust companies wouldn't take a client worth under $25 million. Others might have a separate arm for those special clients.

NEXT MATCH

This seemed like something Perpetual was well placed to handle. There were enough Dick Smiths, Frank Lowys, Marcus Blackmores and Harry Trigaboffs around to sink a ship and most of them would already have very fixed arrangements, but below that level there was clearly a layer of many successful business people, often with more recent wealth, who made up a strong market. Also, we had good connections with Deloitte, KPMG, Gadens, PwC and others to create first class daisy chains to hook some big fish. I liked to think of it as "Perpetual's Suite of Services for the Upper Crust".

I had the advantage of being able to quietly test the waters with some potential partners, on my broad idea prior to any detail being formed, due to my membership of Sydney City Rotary and its mandatory weekly lunchtime meetings attended by many key players in the business community. Also through my contacts created by Perpetual's in-house luncheons with hand-picked guests which my staff arranged on a monthly basis throughout the year. Talking with a few key people showed there was enough mild interest and I put some initial work into how we could set up such a service – a separate wing with the right people to capably deal with those big clients and handle the service mix with our business partners, as well as integration of a more refined service approach within our dedicated investment team.

As something that might have worked or at least was worthy of a serious trial, the concept did not get far. It was understood clearly enough, but the prospect of having to significantly rearrange our investment staff area when everyone was already fully engaged and business flow remained at good levels seemed too daunting. That we already had many wealthy clients on our books, who might lead to others, also appeared to leave management satisfied and comfortable. Agent of change in an industry not looking to change. Again.

~

The second thing that interested me from that US trip was more grass roots. Everyone knows your best targets can often be current customers. No secrets why, but they are easiest to reach.

I had been impressed at the conference with a stirring presentation by Robert Boyle from a trust company in California that was making a difference in the industry – the lucrative funds under management part by sheer size. He drove his company from the marketing seat hard at the primary target of current customers, enlisting the frontline troops copybook style. Every soldier in every one of dozens of offices had the necessary personal contact with every single customer. Visits, phone calls and so on. Day in, day out.

With the authority of the top of the tree he was let loose to not ask but direct all customer personnel to get on board with the strategy to maximise FUM opportunity. No slackers or guys lacking confidence. Do it – and see the supervisors don't stand back but sit on every shoulder and pitch in themselves. The point I make here is that his board and senior management above him were fully involved in seeing that nothing stood in his way. Any problems and he could count on their active support.

In Robert Boyle's world, after a short period of retraining where needed, the fear of tyranny and upsetting clients very quickly evaporated as fresh money rolled in. He started with his mantra "Always ask for the money" and went on from there with his story. Whatever you were doing with the customer, do that then launch. Don't go the other way and end the call hoping the customer will consider and perhaps come back with more business.

Don't ask them to consider, ask for the money. Ask them is that all they have. Have no fear. Expect them to see you only want the company to be of most help to them, nothing else. Be sure they see that in how you approach. Don't wait for an opportunity when they next call or come in. Get the files and make a list. Plan for so many calls per day. You won't catch every fish, but money will happen and it did. Wife needs to check with husband – fine, but don't leave it there. Fix the time to call her back.

You can see it, I'm sure. But it doesn't stop there. How about others in your family? Your friends? Who else do you know that we can help? He had all the psychology down pat and the energy, fuelled by success, plus the authority to make the whole machine work.

I still remember his story about visiting an office in Santa Ana and walking around talking to staff. It went like this:

Just then the phone rang and Julia picked it up. I heard her deal with the client's call and she was about to hang up. She was already up to speed with doing as much as she could for clients. So that was OK.

NEXT MATCH

But I whispered to her, "Before you go, by the way, do you know anyone else we may be able to help?" She repeated those exact words to the client and guess what? I saw she began writing names, got to about eight and was ready to thank the client and end the call.

I stopped her again and whispered, *"Ask for the phone numbers."* And guess what? I saw her begin to write down the phone numbers.

Guess what? Julia became one of our top achievers by the end of the year!

Robert got a standing ovation when he walked off stage. Not an unusual thing to see in other conferences for the tech industry and elsewhere. But in the trust industry it was a powerful sign of what might be possible even on a limited scale, considering the billions of dollars sitting out there waiting and a captive audience of current clients giving you the opportunity to reach them personally.

Well, I brought that back to Perpetual and was determined to put it to work. I could run one-day groups in all the states, talk about the scope of opportunity and how to meet it. And marshal all the troops. But could the supervisors follow up? Or would they be happy just to leave it to marketing? Most likely the latter unless orders to them came from above. Soft acquiescence maybe, but any firm direction to follow the program was hard to see happening any day soon.

The choice was to bin the whole concept or try to find a way to give it a try. I did that by talking it over with Hugh Whitmore, a friend at management consultancy WDScott, and engaged him because I knew he presented well and had all the necessary attributes to speak our language and hopefully persuade some in our audience. Perpetual would pay for somebody else to do exactly what I could have done, but hopefully this way would make it stick as far as possible.

We set up sessions in every state to build confidence that a positive approach in the client's interest would be well received and to show that everyone could easily do the job and that good results were entirely within reach. Every staff member having some client contact was covered in a month. A few believers came out of that mission, but hardly anyone asked about results and although managers went through the motions of following through, they showed little of the energy necessary to fuel the program. Agent of change – don't get in the way.

Let me give you one more story to further demonstrate the role marketing can play, although it became another missed opportunity for Perpetual.

A very impressive developer, Tony Baldwin, had developed the beautiful Bayview Gardens retirement village on Sydney's northern beaches which, as it grew to some 250 residences, became something of a model in the early stages of the retirement village industry. Its board was carefully formed to enhance its standing in the community, with several people such as Averill Fink of the Council on the Ageing as board members. I also became a board member since Perpetual was trustee within trust deeds which were part of lease arrangements for all the residents, and I clearly saw the scope for us to help many with their investment affairs, in many cases considerable, as well as estate planning.

To succeed required a relatively simple approach of inviting residents to information evenings in the Village, presentations by our skilled people including performance of our common funds and forming closer connections that could then be followed up. But discussion within management again met little interest. Residents knew us through the trust deeds and would come to us if they wanted any help. Besides that, such events would put some of our key investment staff in a position of having to engage in follow-ups and sell to warm prospects – and they were all fully occupied handling the business of existing clients.

Eventually I began to feel that I had gone as far as I could in creating changes that would be of any real significance in the Perpetual group. Our image was fine and the usual marketing support was good with my small team of good people around the country, but beyond that Perpetual was set on its own course and offered little further challenge for me.

In closing this chapter, I must say Perpetual was a fine organisation then, and still is. And from the sidelines I can see it has come some way since those days of my tenure. I believed we could have done more, but perhaps I wanted to believe their promise at the beginning that they were willing to change or assumed they understood what I had meant back then. Maybe it's just that I felt things could change faster with a marketing additive in the tank.

Lion eats zebra

We're heading back to the CBC for this next story, which happened after I had left the bank. I don't know who left the kitchen door unlocked at bedtime, but if I had still been around things might (or most likely wouldn't) have been a bit different. I was gone a year before the fan got clogged.

The merger with the National Bank impacted some 20,000 lives including families, but might have been different with just a shade of marketing common sense.

Hopefully you'll see the point that when any firm is going down and there is no parachute, all the people in the plane must accept the inevitable. In this case the venerable old CBC was not falling. Acquisitions are part of life and in lots of cases they enable growth to benefit mankind, bringing new things to more people around the globe, enabling improvements. Even greater efficiencies so that an organisation can do better as a resource in matching supply to demand. Here it was just about money, pure and simple. No better helping hand up for the underprivileged. No improvement in what people wanted and couldn't get. One might question the morality of such cases and the old maxim of shareholders' interest plays its part. But here money came before the lives of so many. Greater opportunities for all? Pull the other leg!

The key to doing it all properly was our missing in action hero: marketing.

To be fair, execution of the merger took its time and lots of staff kept their jobs as the branch network was slowly rearranged; some even got more bars on their epaulettes. But it was still a tectonic shift in what everyone was used to and relied on as a visible career path in the CBC tradition. The thousands of good CBC people I had known would have carried on, adjusted and kept a cheerful face, wonderful professional people as they were then and still are – as I meet up with some of them now in our remarkable CBC Officers Club, an institution and a story in itself.

The big bank, the National, had been stalking the not so little bank, CBC, for years. At one or two points the National Bank was told to slink off back to its lair. Then the time came when it pounced and captured its prey. The CBC and all who sailed in her got swallowed and the message to all the crew was don't ask questions because the answers are locked in the strongroom at the other place, maybe with cartons of lazy ammo on the top shelf there. Just be assured that nobody loses, jobs will remain, career paths will still have the lights turned on.

Also, who cared about the two million CBC customers who would be told that soon they would be banking with someone else? No options given other than their choice of walking if they weren't happy.

Now here's an interesting bit. Everyone knew that people often banked somewhere partly for the loyalty factor: "I've always banked there and so did my father and they've always treated us fairly." In lots of cases it was a main reason for the widely held belief that all banks are the same. To some extent it's the same today. People stay. People move when things happen. Habit/inertia.

Meanwhile what was happening over at ANZ, Commonwealth and Westpac? Did any of their people wake up one night and think this is an opportunity to get a great message out to a prime target along lines of: "Now that you're having to switch to the National, why not come over and see what we can do for you?" Two million-plus prospects. Not too optimistic we could pick up another four or six percent market share if we gave it a go. But no. Nothing. It was the same as far as I know with earlier takeovers involving ES&A Bank, the other Commercial Bank, the Rural. Let the buyer take the spoils and good luck to them. We're fine about it. Business is good.

We'll return to the merger in a moment, but just reflect on that missed marketing opportunity. Still today why is it hard to see much marketing thrust in finance? With fund managers you might have agents swinging more cash your way if you set their commission a tiny bit above what they can get by putting clients' money elsewhere. But aside from promising performance and having a name that suggests some ancestry to Westminster or other hallowed ground what else? Maybe tell everyone that two of the directors once worked for Goldman Sachs (then again if they're so good, why aren't they still there?). Or get the logo more familiar by more spending on billboards and regular ads in *The Financial Review*. Or sponsoring something.

It's hard in many industries to clarify what we in McCanns defined as "the difference that makes a difference" – the thing to promote as the reason to choose. The company's USP, unique selling proposition. Perhaps even harder for a managed fund (and dangerous to use last year's performance or worse, to make promises, as we all know). Good challenge for any marketer in finance – and if you hit a brick wall, find a way to reshape the place or your products to create a meaningful difference.

That said, marketing has other dimensions as we will see in this "lion eats zebra" story.

Yeah right! So, we should all leave the spice ship and jump aboard the pirate boat? That or walk the plank. No choice, it's a merger. Leave it all to us.

They were super smart in the lions' den too. The protest movement hadn't yet become a way of life and even if it had, no one was going to demonstrate against this. The army over the hill was just like theirs below staff sergeant level. Not the type to revolt over the rising price of ice cream. Or people like we see now who get a brain snap if someone whispers on their shoulder about giving them a bit of a hand up with their lives. Not the life with the twenty-two ladies all swaying to Peer Gynt. No. This one here. Now. "Rack off. No-one's going to tell me how to use my gift of A Precious Life on Earth. I'm in the driver's seat so unbuckle and step out! Imagine. Someone else wanting to take over. No way, mate."

Petitioning wouldn't happen either, they knew. If someone started one it would have gone from paper to parchment by the time it did full circle, petitions not being digitised back then. Not even a couple dozen people in Flinders Street or Martin Place to do a protest. Too much spread. The others couldn't get there with their placards until at least next Tuesday, maybe later.

Now if I had been around and we still had Geoffrey and if he had stopped me in the corridor to ask my opinion… who knows what might have happened? As it was our proud old CBC was stopped in its tracks with the Monkey Blood Pink signs all scrapped. Thousands of people changed hats and moved on and hardly anyone talked about disruption. Signed off. Done. Move along everyone. Pick up your lives. We're looking after you.

A fly on the wall when the titans of commerce met over tea with their invited guests might have noticed nobody had a marketing cap on when all the figures were spread across the big table like in a war room. Profits in one box. Cost savings in another. Efficiency. Tax. Structures. Legal. Systems. Undue Diligence. Tangible Asset Values. Mandatory this and Discretionary that. Write offs. Regulations as to capital. Retirement provisions. Loan risk ratios. Even share of total market.

All of that was just mopping up to confirm the decision already made in principle. Losing benefits built up through years of investing in the CBC image was spilt milk. The brand evaporated and momentum was shafted.

The marketing point to make amid all this is that someone taking a half-brick into the room with the titans might have persuaded them a better path would have been to forget egos and the convincing financials and consider the extra potential in *capitalising* on the CBC's image – not to mention its strength, customer loyalty, staff morale and all the rest – by having the two banks operate side by side under the same ownership. As opposed to destroying one.

Did the analysts who did the audit (if any) three years after the buyout report in detail on the success of the venture? It went smoothly, tick. Heap of cost savings, tick. Bigger slice of the market pie, tick. What might have happened if we ran two banks separately to capitalise on momentum and value already built in each? Hmm. That's a bit harder to sort out. Sorry.

I wonder if the CBC takeover had anything to do with what happened years later when Westpac merged with St George Bank. They're both still ticking along nicely, each with its own slice of the market but in the same family. Marketing!

Getting the board on board

Some directors have come up the hard way. Accounting. Law. Chemical engineering. Geology, Arts or Music. People get jobs in what are new worlds for them not because they were crack biochemists or won last year's award for best architecture in the coffee shops or aircraft hangars category, but for a proven capacity to learn and adapt. We all know that. But it is vital to be sure in your finance board whether everyone sees the complete marketing concept well beyond just the usual promotion or if you need to work on them to get to that level.

You can't pull them into the ring with the textbook marketing presentations in a world where change isn't on the to-do list. They'll give you the nod on the budget figure and leave you to it. I must concede that boards have changed since my early days, but there is always the possibility not everyone will see the full picture because finance is such an intangible.

In finance you can count customers and their worth today, but what effect has any investment in marketing had on your customer base? It's all a different scene without that need where you must commit to producing or importing three thousand tractors by year's end, work out shipping and warehousing and distributors. Get it wrong and there's trouble. Same for toothpaste. Disaster if it's perishables as in decay or progress in styles for fashion.

In my view finance doesn't demand such close scrutiny against effort and that can lead to general acceptance, but less energetic input from a board even with best intentions. You don't want your board to just be happy to go along with you. That might be easy, but there are two ways your board can help: it can provide good input and it can have a strong influence on others in your management team, including those less supportive of your initiatives.

The composition of your finance board may include some directors with experience in consumer goods or other fields who are therefore more attuned to practical marketing.

A wise approach, however, is to assume that's not the case and you need to do some work to get their attention and interest. Beyond just listening because you come across as the executive with the marketing background. For that reason, I digress to tell the following brief story. I'm also telling it because it shows yet another element in the wide spectrum of marketing: how to think clearly and recognise the triggers to effectively reach your market and carefully develop your approach.

Whenever I did the welcome introductions at Perpetual's "Gathering of Investors", held occasionally out in the suburbs, before bringing on the investment team I used to say there are three things a good financial adviser must have. First, look good. Second, be able to speak well. Third, have the right investment knowledge and skillset (one part being honesty).

I said that to try to get our victims' attention and underline that we at Perpetual were exactly the right kind of people they should take advice from and get help from.

Also, I wanted to help them see beyond the guy's nice hair or how friendly the lady was who came and talked to them on Tuesdays after bridge. No, she wasn't going out of her way to where they played bridge, right on time. No need to thank her. The boss at Ords sent her. Go where the pickings are. Better we go to them than hoping they'll drift in through our door.

You might see the Robert Boyle playbook in action here. Step one: somebody is on the Ord Minnett books. Just one person there. OK, answer her questions, meet her needs, then ask, "And who else do you know who we might be able to help?" Step two: get the names or kick the conversation along a bit and up comes a gem about meeting for bridge every Tuesday. On your way to the goldfields.

That's marketing as the driver; if not, it's just serve the customer and next customer please. Wait for business to come to you. Which it won't or maybe will in a trickle.

As I spoke about what *not* to focus on, I could always see a few people nodding as they looked at me. They knew that finding an adviser was scary. Too many who would shunt you and your money this way or that, mostly for the obvious reasons. Perpetual was not like that, and the critical thing is asset choices and allocations and clear objectives for your money and your future. Not the tricks of the trade by looking good and talking well and getting people to like you and therefore believe what you're telling them.

The bottom line here is tell (don't ask) the board to listen to you, not because you've got the marketing cap and it's your turn in the line of presenters for the day but to use logic and common sense and to comprehend the meaning and purpose of your presentation. The board needs to understand your purpose, not just employ you. Then you've got them with their oars in the water. Importantly, you'll also have the authority to better execute your plans, particularly when you meet other pockets of resistance within the company as you inevitably will.

The open road

In my field and on the path of being an agent of change as opposed to being head of marketing for cheese, lip balm, car tyres or mobile phones (where no agent of change need apply for the position because there isn't one) it was natural to broaden my vision. Which included consulting. A dream way to try sometime because I'd be able to apply my skills where there was fertile ground, get a contract and do the job. Then get the ten thousand for two weeks' work and exit without being tied down in a place that may not have suited me.

I used to say in doing that the first part would be learning everything I needed to know then showing up with a list of eleven things the company had to get right to achieve what it said it wanted to achieve. Always there would be eight they could do quite easily. It was the other three that would be a problem, unlikely to be handled right or with a commitment of steel. "Thanks. Great work and leave those other three for us to get onto as and when we can!" Mostly those remaining three were the real keys to winning much more than the other eight easy things.

Leading the horse to water and making it drink sounds familiar. "But this is what you paid me for. Not just the simple solutions to parts of the whole, but to drill down on the harder changes that are so critical." Sounds like fun and using my life instead of it using me.

So I became a consultant specialising in financial services marketing and quickly found opportunities. Lined up a few assignments and scheduled them in through the next six months, leaving enough room to sell my services to others. There was no problem making more than enough to pay the bills and it looked like I was set. The flexibility was good and bad. Intense work some weeks to satisfy clients with critical timing, sometimes several at once. Golf three times another week. Meeting deadlines regardless of holidays. I remember one year spending the whole of Easter writing up the templates for marketing seminars for second-tier public servants in Canberra in the cabin of our boat in Refuge Bay while Elaine and the kids drifted around in the dinghy or went swimming.

That one was due to Paul Keating, treasurer in the Hawke government at the time, deciding that some, but not all, government departments needed to be "commercialised" as in operating as a business and accountable for the bottom line. I met dozens of highly professional senior people when I conducted those seminars (groups of twelve again as per the guidebook) and it would have been interesting to see how that all unfolded. Probably some good came out of it in improved control, better decision-making, and cost efficiency as politics and the world moved on.

My own boss for once. Deciding my own pace. No anxiety about loss of security of tenure. Perfect, since by that time we had moved to our new house at Palm Beach on Sydney's northern beaches with the boat on its mooring in Pittwater out the front. I enjoyed the freedom of consulting for just over a year and then one afternoon the phone rang.

Out of the frying pan

It was Kevin Barry in a recruiting firm. I hadn't crossed paths with him for ten years or so. He told me that the new Australian Stock Exchange (ASX) was almost fully set up and running after government legislation in 1987 enabled the six state stock exchanges to become one national market, but it needed a marketing manager. Someone who would know the ropes and fit in. And with enough diplomatic skills to cope with the animals. He said a number of people had been interviewed without success and he knew I had done well at the CBC and thought I would be the man. Funny how your past catches up with you.

A couple of meetings at the ASX included the tensions attached to a Sydney head office and how that went down in Melbourne (they partly settled that by putting a couple of departments down there). Also, the risk of a stranglehold on ASX management because everyone in the broking community felt they owned the exchange and therefore knew best how to run it. Enough red flags to make anyone nervous, but I decided maybe a new way to make a name for myself with some sort of public achievement. Not the first battle I had leaped into. And what's more, what did I have to lose?

The first day at my office in what had been the Sydney Stock Exchange and was now the ASX came with several very professional staff and all the physical comforts. But the highlight of that day was meeting the chairman, Laurie Cox from Potter Warburg Securities based in Melbourne. A great leader and very likeable. We chatted as I accompanied him to some meeting down the hall and he put it on the line. If he saw the media anywhere printing or saying "Sydney Stock Exchange" three months from today that would be the end of my job. Period.

We had the corporate identity manual complete with the stationery for all the states in different colours to appease the factions and obviously get it over the line, which we quickly scrapped (the colours) and the ASX label was on everything, neat and tidy. But you know journos with ten stories all happening at once, old habits and deadlines to meet. You can't just send out a notice to everyone saying, "Please use this name from now on." Watch out for storms.

Second day. Airline strike all week and maybe longer. I decided a good move might be to show my face to the Melbourne natives so, unable to fly of course, I booked a bus seat and sat up all night to get to Melbourne for breakfast on my third day, Wednesday morning. Then to our office to chat with Neil Beaumont, who became my best right-hand man ever, and to meet his local marketing team. He'd lined up half a dozen brokers to come over after lunch. After a pleasant chat around the table one asked, "And how often will you be coming to Melbourne, Bruce?" to which I replied as often as needed, no problem. I added a casual comment that the only thing I couldn't do was to relocate there because I lived in a place called Palm Beach. I repeated, just to be clear: whenever they needed me, I'd be down like a shot.

A day or two later my boss, Gavin Campbell, called to tell me that Laurie had called him from his den in Melbourne saying I had told the brokers down there they wouldn't be seeing much of me in Melbourne. Nice people. They couldn't have cared less about my sacrifice sitting up on the bus all night just to show them my commitment. Snakes in the grass. More grenades would be lobbed my way over the next five years and I soon realised they came with the territory. Besides, I'd pitched my tent in new countries before and somehow survived.

Brokers. Lots so remarkably pleasant and friendly that it was hard to spot the wolves in sheep's clothing. On another occasion, in Perth, the head of one firm chose to big-note himself by giving me, in front of about thirty of his staff, some blunt messages that I needed to take back to Sydney about how the ASX should be run. Or Perth would go back to having its own exchange.

The ASX Investor Centres I had inherited from each of the state stock exchanges had libraries for the public to help them find every listed company's announcement since year dot, books to browse and buy on investing, and staff to satisfy queries about the exchange and the market. ASX Open Days brought in good crowds each year. All of it was popular and supported the concept of a transparent stock exchange. You couldn't not provide some sort of service to the public or there'd be riots, calls from Canberra, stoning of brokers' cars (you might wish) and so on. Meanwhile the gallery above the deafening, chaotic trading floor was home to those investors who carried earplugs and could watch the chalkies and follow their stocks. More for day-traders than mums and dads.

I had my day in the sun, if you could call it that, by presenting to the monthly board meetings, to show them charts from research and to explain or support some change being put forward. The meeting I most clearly remember, however, was the battle over my Investor Centres.

The ASX was not making huge profits in those early days with high system costs a major hurdle and there was talk in the camp about getting rid of the Investor Centres everywhere. My twelve cost centres making up the whole operation with about seventy staff and costly leased floor space in all the states. The proportion of the adult population owning shares at that time was less than twenty percent. Laurie was at the meeting, appearing to be open on the issue but waiting to see how the rest of the board felt. I couldn't know which way he might go, good chair. Gavin too. Of the other directors all were brokers except John Barnard who also served on the Coles board. The weight of opinion after a long thirty minutes or so was clearly in favour of scrapping the Investor Centres as a needless and costly arm of the exchange.

The nub from the brokers was that they made their money from the institutions and other holders of big portfolios and servicing little people was a costly pain in the backside in every broking house. You made no money from them although the board had heard me often enough talk about attracting a bigger share of the public into share investing. I was marketing "share investment" as an alternative to other avenues, which anyone could see was to the ultimate benefit of the ASX. But they didn't want my opinion.

John Barnard sorted that. He was always energetic and pro-active and he got their attention when the smoke started to clear. Gave all the reasons for retail, many obvious, some under the radar. The verdict: Investor Centres could stay. Music to my ears you might say.

Doing the rounds of brokers more or less constantly I'd often ask why well-known stockbroker and entrepreneur Rene Rivkin was the only one in the daily news finance slot talking up the value of investing in shares. Rene, standing out in the broking world but, as some said, living on the edge (years later he was convicted of insider trading and lost his broking licence). The brokers immediately put focus on the charming Rene and didn't hear a scrap of what I was suggesting. No surprise. We're too busy with clients to take a call from the Nine Network to meet us in Bond Street with our jackets on and the make-up girl ready to straighten our ties. Don't you dare give them our numbers.

Around the same time, I commissioned Towers Perrin, a highly reputable global firm in the broad investment services sector, to undertake a study into the performance of various forms of investment over the previous ten years, considering all costs and tax effects – shares, property, fixed interest and cash. The results were published as an ASX Investments Report with bar charts showing long-term return as well as average annual return before and after tax at low and highest rates. It also explained all the factors used as a complete and fair basis of the calculations as well as mentioning basic shares/property differences such as easier conversion of assets back to cash, when needed, in the case of shares. My directions to Towers Perrin were to avoid the risk of accusations of bias, such as might arise if figures on share or property prices were too selective and could appear they were used to get the result we wanted. Share investing came out on top by a small margin, enough to support any promotion encouraging people to consider what to do with their money at that time when wealth was noticeably expanding.

My two-page printed report using the Towers Perrin stamp for credibility was circulated to the broking community as useful ammunition. I had deliberately kept it concise and clear to enable the widest possible readership and use. Some firms mentioned it in their newsletters to clients and it attracted useful media attention. I used it in the Investor Centres too.

Showing the ASX Investments Report to the board, however, was almost a non-event, despite me letting them know, two months earlier, that we were producing it and explaining its purpose. Little comment from the board members. No serious questions and certainly no discussion about how it might be used to good effect, now that they could see the final product, as an ongoing authoritative item of reference to encourage more people into share investing. I had expected at least some excitement over this new tool, which was quite different to most other material being put out that relied on picking certain stocks, and wondered if the board's rather passive view had anything to do with the fact that almost all the directors belonged to different broking firms and so were competing with one another. Or just their limited interest in small investors.

Beyond the ASX board, it seemed that few brokers saw the report as a way to jump in and help Rene in his one-man quest to tell ordinary people about the benefits of investing in shares. There seemed little reason to keep it alive by having Towers Perrin do constant updates so that the media would become used to giving it regular exposure.

Soon after, the initial plans from the inception of the ASX to close the trading floors began to take firm shape. Obvious natural progression into the new digital world. The order came to my desk: find a way to replace the trading floors. We still needed to have a face. Yes, for the public. The ordinary small investor until then had little hope of following live prices from public galleries over trading floors in every state unless they could handle the chaos below. Things were finally changing.

In short order I presented the solution in the form of Trans-Lux LED screens and a support mechanism to complete the package. Software by the distributor Trade Centre Products to interconnect with our data source systems and run displays in any configuration required with guaranteed ongoing support. Great product all round.

The whole world of investing was maturing and expanding sideways because people directly owning shares in listed companies were steadily increasing in number. So too was their stake through the growing array of investment vehicles. More and more customers and with financial advisers growing like weeds everywhere pushing the lorry down the road. Ownership as a percentage of people had more than doubled since the ASX's year dot and my initially agreed five-year term was at its halfway point.

Then came the biggest moment in my life up to that point. My wonderful, classy Elaine, never a sick day in her life, was diagnosed with cancer. Incurable. People everywhere know the pain. It went on for the next two years and Elaine, because of who she was, helped us all, Louise Tim and me, through that time with her dignity and so much courage. Not one day or moment of complaint. So many of her friends who admired, respected and loved her saw that too. We are forever grateful for that, my Elaine.

I learned a lot from that period in my life. About what things matter. How to appreciate the gift that each of us has been given, see our true values and use our finite time and abilities in the best way possible. And help others do the same. It was a painful time and those next two years turned my life upside down, but I had the constant support of so many friends and all the wonderful people in the stock exchange for which I will always be grateful. With my five-year term coming to its end, I chose to set off to discover fresh ground. More on that after this next chapter.

At the casino with your money

This chapter is about hedge funds, which might seem out of place in a finance career story, but my time in Perpetual and the stock exchange gave me some insight into hedge fund practices and their effect on ordinary investors and listed companies. As the chapter title suggests, people need to know how their money is used – or misused. There is another reason for its inclusion: understanding hedge funds brings into view scope for marketing to create opportunities and, of greater significance, the role marketing could play in disrupting the whole industry.

The stock exchange rule prohibiting short selling makes it very clear. Brokers must not accept sell orders from clients who cannot deliver those shares to buyers on settlement.

As we all watch markets, share prices move constantly due to the actions of various participants. Investors, fund managers and day traders who, in the sense that they are betting on the market, include hedge funds.

The difference with hedge funds is their intention to cause price movements well beyond the range of normal trading, legally manipulating prices for quick gains through short-term selling and re-buying. That much is no secret. Listed companies and shareholders have no choice but to suffer and accept the situation.

A closer look into hedge funds, where that may be possible, will show some who have substantial shareholdings in their own right and others who own few shares and rely on their ability to acquire them only for short periods to conduct their business involving shares in a targeted company. Note that such business necessarily involves trading substantial numbers to be certain of creating a desired fall in a share price and it would rarely be safe for a hedge fund to use its own money to buy those shares to sell them and drive down their value. A self-defeating exercise at any time. So the only option is to *borrow* the shares from owners willing to lend them with the understanding that, by doing so, there will be a fall in asset value.

It doesn't take much imagination to see that most owners of substantial holdings of shares, that is private investors and corporations, will not lend parts of their holdings to hedge funds. In my career I have spoken to many who confirmed this. The only avenue available to hedge funds then appears to be fund managers and it cannot be known how many of those owners of huge portfolios participate in the practice. It's likely to be many, perhaps it's even common practice, and the only reason they do it is to earn fees from such short-term lending. On top of the fees they get from you for looking after your money and growing your wealth.

Can it be legal for any fund manager to use assets it holds on your behalf, from the money you have invested, in such a way that some reduction in value is virtually certain? When the fund manager has attracted your money on its commitment to preserve and grow your wealth?

Whilst this practice is questionable from a moral point of view, it's made possible through the mechanism of a mandatory trust deed for a managed fund, mentioned earlier in this book in the chapter about Perpetual, and its published product disclosure statement (PDS). Look carefully and you may find something in any fund manager's PDS about being able to use its assets in ways it may see fit. The fact that you have been given the PDS and have supposedly read through it before placing your money with the fund manager ties up any loose ends.

Nobody can know the exact amount of fees hedge funds pay to fund managers where short term lending of shares is carried out. But it would be considerable, considering both the sheer size of any one transaction needed to cause any price fall and the extent of hedge fund operations throughout any given year. Fund managers depend on client fees, but other income earned by using your assets can be considerable – acceptable even, except for the fact that in using your assets those assets are subsequently reduced in value. The extent of such falls in value may in an overall sense be absorbed amid all the daily rises and falls in the market and any incident of lending a particular parcel of shares, however large, for a short period, just becomes another element in the totality of any fund manager's huge portfolio worth many millions. In that sense, we need not be overly concerned. The good that fund managers do outweighs the smaller things. The end justifies the means. But it is still a nefarious practice not widely understood or talked about.

The stock exchange of course benefits from hedge fund operations since its income comes from trading. Brokers also gain considerably. The proportion of all sharemarket trading attributable to hedge funds can only be guessed at and, in a similar vein, there seems no way anyone can ascertain what proportion of a fund manager's income, as part of overall reported profits in any year, comes from working with hedge funds.

Brokers and, I must say the ASX itself, have a common view: that it helps market liquidity. Others clearly see things differently. Listed companies rarely, if ever, see that trading in their shares by private investors and institutions needs any such activity to boost the liquidity of their shares. But it's a global practice and seems to be an integral part of how markets operate, finding ways to use markets for some participants at the expense of others.

Discussing this with others over the years, including one or two politicians, has naturally turned to possible solutions on some occasions, which are unlikely to ever happen but remain practical. I referred earlier to trust deeds for all managed funds being a legal requirement. In the same vein, legislation could be introduced with certain changes stipulating that by year-end trust deeds governing managed funds must contain clear conditions that assets held on behalf of investing clients cannot be lent or provided in any way to third parties for any purpose. To apply to all managed funds, not just new entrants to the field. That would be policed through the process of formal audits carried out every year with penalties applying to auditors and company executives found to be breaking the rules.

I could go on about how hedge funds enhance their plans to drive prices down by creating so-called independent analyst reports against prices of individual stocks; the immediacy demanded by their operations due to the risks of being caught out between sell and buy actions; and such things as plays going south after some unanticipated extraordinary event. But what I have outlined here should be enough.

As promised earlier, there are marketing aspects that emerge in this story.

The first is that there can be opportunity for a smart fund manager to take advantage of the situation with a strategy to increase public awareness of how hedge funds and their competitors work together to affect asset values (against clients' general expectations about the safety of their money) and then capitalising on that by strong public relations and advertising – not only to its clients but to the broader market of all investors. Making clear that it has firm policies not to engage in such practices. An interesting new story for the media, always seeking new subjects. Being first would be a natural advantage and while others might follow, the effect of the strategy would obviously be to attract business from everyone having fresh concerns about where their money is invested – at a time when more and more people are taking an active interest in the subject of money, particularly their money. New business and better market share for a fund manager willing to step up may well offset any potential income it might have otherwise received through hedge funds.

One final comment on this story, no less important from a marketing viewpoint. "Disruption" is a relatively new phenomenon in commercial life around the world, particularly in technology. But one should not overlook the scene in circles where technology plays a lesser part or no part at all. Our entire money market, remember, is much bigger than every single market for products of any kind and it is conditioned to respond to moves and changes much more than in past years just because there are so many more options for buying or doing anything now. It is ripe for further change when something like I describe in this story, even without legislative action, might take place, creating market awareness in the process and resonating with everyone in the market, to the point where many will alter their behaviour.

Freedom

With "agent of change" stamped on the back of my jersey and having played my game at the stock exchange, the time seemed right to take a break and find my next opportunity, or to create one as it turned out.

Leaving the ASX was not a signal for me to retire. I recognised that I had some assets with my standing in the broking community, which would help open doors, and with my understanding of how LED screens could be valuable in that target market and how data could be configured and used in various applications. Other things too like how to sell, and just confidence. Which goes a long way.

Trade Centre Products (TCP), who sold the ASX its new trading screens and software, knew me well and I knew them and the Trans-Lux product. As with many distributors who represent lots of brands and products, it was natural for them not to carry the cost of a substantial sales resource. You could say TCP was more of an order-taker. Not without a good sales function, but with limited scope to work fresh fields.

I talked with TCP about what I might be able to do for them and perhaps as expected met the issue that they couldn't or wouldn't cut their margins to make room for me to get any return attached to results for my sales efforts. Poker hands maybe. The common funds story all over again.

My only option if I wanted to use this opportunity was therefore to add an extra margin on sales to pay me for introducing new business. Worth a try because I saw that Trans-Lux could be sold on highest quality, capitalising on the ASX installations in all Australian states and penetration so far in dealing rooms everywhere. As well as the TCP backup of software and ongoing support. I knew that the market had deep pockets and would buy on quality not price. Add in reliable performance; you can't have your data falling off the screens any day of the week or even once in a blue moon. Deal done. I would be paid by tacking on that extra margin.

My first six months brought me nothing. Not one dollar. But I worked on and the pot warmed up. Fast forward another few months and it settled into a good business with another benefit of increasing value to me – freedom.

Being now a solo traveller, I could take time off at my discretion knowing that TCP would be able to close and execute whenever a sale came off the conveyor belt. Nobody bought in a flash. Discussions, follow ups, meetings, proposals submitted and having to be pushed up the chain for the final tick. It all took time. You could never know when a sale might come through whether I was downing a Guinness in Ireland, improving my Italian in Perugia or getting sand in my boots in the Simpson Desert.

During trips I checked out stock exchanges in other cities and also saw what Trans-Lux did in the US – from opening the crates as they arrived from China to assembling the LED chips into modules for shipping to Trans-Lux in other countries where the screens went through final assembly into tailored frames to order, some the size of cricket ground sight screens.

All in my own sweet time. No fixed tour of duty as a company executive. Free to wander the planet as I wished while earning a living, subject to the time I spent back at base camp finding targets and following up on prospects. A good way to go.

The directors' chapter

I have a lot of respect and admiration for company directors. I've been one myself. Not in your league, but still a few notches above the level of Bondi Dental Supplies. Your tasks are formidable and the best of you shoulder the burden of captains everywhere with sound wisdom and courage. There is no-one else to step in beside or above you. Everest.

All through writing this book the two main things on my mind were how much the craft of marketing in its broadest sense can lead to great improvements, and how directors are essential to making the most progress through involvement – beyond calling from the sidelines and replacing players or the coach.

I have tried to help explain where directors can fit into the marketing frame particularly in financial organisations and you may see I've tried constructive criticism rather than a full-frontal attack – that's not my style. I'm not vicious. Except for that incident at Coolum, Queensland, on the twelfth hole, long ago now. I never touched his ball. And I didn't see him around the course much after that.

In all things finance it's even more important to have a firm grasp on marketing than when you're marketing tangible products. Elsewhere there's that discipline of ensuring a smooth path from factory to end user that demands marketing has a seat at the table. Keep steady and fight it out with the competitors, up the volume on the production line with a new plant in Dandenong. Bring in the robots or tell China to ramp up to 24-hour mode. It's all the same. Not so in the world of financial services.

You're in the pool on a finance board because you take your job seriously; in the mix with others, some you knew from university days, and besides, you know business back to front. That's all great, but focus on marketing is even more critical in finance because you already have customers in hand. Unlike most other places where yesterday's customers have paid up and gone. Some customers will return, but those companies need constant marketing just to keep their market position. They can't just depend on organic growth. And neither can your finance board as the competitive world keeps changing.

You're working for the owners and quite a lot of them take as much proprietorial interest as renters in a strata block as long as the share price plays follow-the-leader northwards and the half-yearly dividends come into the bank, preferably franked. However, others are watching like a tiger in the ferns. You might hold the annual general meeting in Ulladulla on the NSW south coast or Perth on Christmas Eve, but some shareholders will still come and occasionally ask questions related to marketing. How much the company invests. What it gets in return.

Being able to respond to shareholders is important, but that's just the tip. The real iceberg is your power to play a huge part in ensuring your company has a marketing culture, seeing through consistent involvement that marketing strategies and plans actually work, that changes happen to create and meet opportunities – and that your executives follow through and are fully committed. It's marketing over finance, not finance over marketing, and more stakeholders see that today than in the past. Macquarie shows it knows that. Commonwealth Bank too. Some others I'd mark a bit lower and others lower still. Meanwhile the market swells and more opportunities emerge for directors to help get a bigger slice by understanding and being smart with marketing.

In my journey I must say that I rarely found directors unfriendly. I think some grew up with the principle that they should keep on good terms with the executives just as we may have learned not to get directors offside. Of course, it would be naïve to think some didn't have inner thoughts about things and a few would present challenges through opposite views, sometimes useful and at other times needing debate. In thinking of a few others who were just difficult, my mind goes back to one in Perth who was fine any morning, but never after lunch. He was well known in local business circles as a morning person.

You might say relations were generally civilised. Kept under control. Manners and mutual respect were sometimes taken for granted but worth remembering. In other circles some have little restraint, using expletives that might set your hair on fire or make a dog cringe. But that wasn't the norm at the board level in my experience in finance. Nor is it my style and I encourage you to go the same way. It does help towards success.

There were many pleasant conversations and most directors were amiable enough. Even when I put them through media training, an experience they didn't exactly cherish, and tried to encourage them to take media calls, such as for a statement from the stock exchange on some event affecting the indices, a system failure or something happening in its broking member community, when the media was frantic to get some comment to complete a news story. Or when I would have to shepherd them into a room for the group photo for the annual report. I used a trick I learned during my early days of getting one of them to say, on my nod, "This is our worst ordeal of the year." Everyone would smile and my photographer would get his shot.

Match point

Earlier on I suggested that there's a lot more to marketing than meets the eye. So don't be mistaken that this book is just some tips and a few amusing or interesting stories. There's a message I hope you'll take from it, worth more than all the technical stuff like matching creative to research findings or comparing clicks to Google spending.

It's simply this. That if you are head of marketing anywhere, or aspire to be, you have two jobs. The first one is easy to understand: take care of all the usual marketing paraphernalia and practise your skills in that. Develop and constantly refine strategy, lead your team, seek accountability for what you do and what you spend. Execute well, as they say.

Your second job is under the radar too often. Hopefully what I've written has helped to shed light on the fact that everything is marketing. As the one with the title, it rests on you more than anyone else to keep the sharpest eye on that "everything" and use your skills to make a difference in the place you call your working home by getting others to improve their vision of the impact you can all have on your customers.

Going to extremes to demonstrate this, imagine that your worker on the factory floor burrs a screw assembling his next dishwasher. Does he let it go or replace the screw? It might cop a scratch going down the ramp to packing and end up in factory seconds, but at least let's try for our quality image where we can. Not help destroy the brand bit by bit like that National Bank kid with his shirt hanging out. Or if your person at the check-in counter is great at her job but can't help getting impatient with a nasty customer, is that OK?

This is just as vital in finance as in the factory and I've used check-in counter examples here because everyone in finance still performs functions that have some effect on customers, your market.

Administration, processing, application of controls, procedures, IT systems. Delivery of your finance product and how well it matches that of the competition and meets customer expectations will always depend on how the company is driven. Every employee needs to recognise that. Effects are visible every day from the customer's viewpoint.

Completion of a transaction, handling enquiries, paperwork, getting to speak with the right person, fourth person in the phone queue, emails you can't reply to. We all suffer at times and it comes down to people, procedures and systems in just the same way as the factory and check-in people. Bright signs emerge when you see one place enabling you to be called back instead of hanging on the line for twelve minutes. Security checks might soon include your blood type. They are needed, but tortuous when you just want to ask one question not even related to your personal affairs, like what date a report is due out. You could say a marketing culture in finance is even more important than for dishwashers because every single customer is so much closer to you.

You can make a difference across the whole company, as its team member responsible for marketing. How? By infiltrating yourself into the structure of your company in ways where you can influence all the other moving parts. The managers and supervisors. The people involved in operation and systems. Just the same as those in other workplaces who can speak to the factory floor worker and the check-in person where you can't. Take that same principle up the line too. The ones that lead the whole army can do better with your help and guidance. Believe that and accept that part of the job will be a lifetime's work, and it'll be worth the effort and your patience.

From my own experience I can tell you there will be times when you won't perceive any change, people being people. But don't give up. It will still give you the inner satisfaction of knowing you're doing something you believe in. Just like Greta and David. Somewhere, over your horizon, what you do will have an effect.

Postscript

I was inspired to write this book by my three very bright grandchildren so that they might one day, when they're interested, know what I got up to in my earlier years.

I also appreciate the words of my wonderful travel writer daughter Louise, who told me that writing helps us to know what we really think. I'd add that it also helps you appreciate what you've done in your life. For me, writing this book has helped me see that I have something to pass on for a better understanding of marketing in the finance world – its wide scope well beyond what many see.

My beautiful partner Rasa has provided further motivation with her boundless energy, positive spirit and belief that your life is what you make it and is shaped by everything you do.

My marketing career has given me so much and I hope reading about some of it will benefit you. Broadly in terms of how organisations function in a marketing sense, and particularly for you if you're choosing to follow a marketing path in your working life.

Meanwhile that old oak tree, the finance industry, remains solid and strong, still growing, impervious to changes in the weather – but it has matured, I'd say. From my experience marketing can make a big difference in how it grows as our world picks up speed at an ever-increasing rate in the future.

www.ingramcontent.com/pod-product-compliance
Lightning Source LLC
Chambersburg PA
CBHW050319010526
44107CB00055B/2317